Not so Little!

THE BOOK OF
DUNG

CAROLINE HOLMES

SUTTON PUBLISHING

First published in 2006 by
Sutton Publishing Limited · Phoenix Mill
Thrupp · Stroud · Gloucestershire · GL5 2BU

British Library Cataloguing in Publication Data
A catalogue record for this book is available from the British Library.

ISBN 0-7509-4051-4

All uncredited pictures are from the author's collection.

Title page engraving: Virgil published his Georgics in four books. The first
deals with tillage and pasturage, the sun rises over a scene of
agricultural activity. Is that a muck heap in the front
left-hand corner?

Typeset in 11/14pt Photina.
Typesetting and origination by
Sutton Publishing Limited.
Printed and bound in England by
J.H. Haynes & Co. Ltd, Sparkford.

CONTENTS

To my sisters

Lizzie and Kate

for the rich humour and fertile minds we share

ACKNOWLEDGEMENTS

It is certainly unusual to be invited to write a book on dung but I must thank Jaqueline Mitchell for the challenge. I have relished fulfilling the commission, helped by a legion of people who have robustly contributed. What to call the end product? I was stuck in a groove of 'Dung-ho', but thanks to a flash of genius from Serena Gosden Hood it was rechristened *The Not so Little Book of Dung*. Rich and ripe thanks to: Peter Clinton, who formally introduced me to the heroic dung beetle; Philip Norman at the Museum of Garden History, whose encyclopedic knowledge of their collections was invaluable; Dr Pat Murrell, awash with lavatorial research, who generously lent me her copious notes, asides and books; and Canon Peter Macleod-Miller, whose manurance of souls and minds incorporates a panoply of well-dunged references. And I owe great gratitude to Andrew Smyth for allowing me to quote extensively from *Caesar's Passage*.

A constant joy of tutoring in continuing education is the wealth of knowledge brought by the students, and especial thanks go to Kate Bryce on France and Theo Stanning on Ingeburg Burchard's work in Kenya. Thanks also to the Lindley Library; University Library, Cambridge; Bury St Edmunds Records Office; Paignton Zoo; and Yvette Cowles, Jane Hutchings and Jane Entrican at Sutton Publishing. Additional gems came from Pat Crocker, Lucy Goodman, Nicky Hartopp, Ramsey Shewell Cooper, John Throssell and Mary Wohlleb – and an Aussie Salute to John Hall.

Lastly, as always, thanks to Erica Hunningher for negotiations and wise counsel, and to my husband David, who has trawled the bookshelves and spent a week's holiday copy reading. Our sons Will and Nick remembered usable trifles and offered a further glossary of terms that were well beyond the remit of this book.

v

What would you define as a family outing? Fabre wrote: 'My sight, which is still fairly good, although exceedingly tired, is aided by the deep-seeing eyes of all my family. I owe to them the fact that I am able to pursue my researches: let me thank them here.'

Part One

TIME AND MOTION

Fertile genius and elegant ornament

A vignette of timeless motion from Bewick's *Quadrupeds*

INTRODUCTION

He soon would learn to think like me,
And bless his ravish'd eyes to see
Such order from confusion sprung,
Such gaudy tulips rais'd from dung.

Jonathan Swift

Dung-ho, a celebration of the perfectly designed package: excretion as enriching creation and creative enrichment. Farflung dung – there's so much more to dung than double-digging and rhubarb-forcers. Where would we be without dung? Constipated – the word conjures up a stale body, a stale mind, stasis, a world in which nothing moves on. Dung is produced in a functional motion that excretes waste in an array of ways and outcomes. Human, animal, fish and insect bodies need to rid themselves of unnecessary digestive bulk, species and diet fashioning the end product. Carnivores leave the least, as meat is a rich source of easily digested nourishment with little waste. Herbivores have to eat almost all the time as plants are less sustaining and less digestible, and such animals tend to have 'straight-through' systems. And, as the seventeenth-century essayist Francis Bacon said: 'Money is like muck, not good except it be spread.'

Dung transforms and uplifts the earth into a green and pleasant land with a modicum of ripe smell. This is a bucolic vision, of course. Rural populations produce acceptable amounts of dung, but translated into an urban setting humans and animals in increasingly confined spaces end up awash in their own excrement. The planet wants, indeed needs, dung but excess excrement produces filth and degradation. However primitive some societies appear, the fundamental human desire to be warm, clean and decent dictates finding shelter where intake is separate from outgoings. To daub someone with excrement reduces them symbolically to dirt. Most animals also keep themselves apart from their excrement – an area of repugnancy – and good husbandry recognises that. The resulting human middens have provided instructive fodder for archaeologists, while animal middens of packrats, woodrats, stick-nest rats and rock badgers have provided evidence of climate and vegetation change.

The Greek word for dung – *kopros* – provides the suffix for the linguistics of dung. Coprolite is commonly known as dinosaur droppings, but watch out for coprolith, a hardened ball of faeces in the bowels, and coprostasis, more commonly known as constipation. This in turn can lead to blood poisoning from trapped faeces, a condition known as copraemia. Coprophilous describes one who is fond of dung, but coprophilia verges on the obscene and approaches the pornographic. The hero of this book is the dung beetle, a coprophagist of utter sagacity, who engages in coprology, eating and gathering dung. This beetle does not suffer from copremesis or stercoraceous vomiting. (Stercutius, incidentally, is the god of ordure.)

In the nineteenth century a branch of medicine called scatology made diagnoses from the study of faeces, although the word today implies little more than robust, well-dunged humour. In researching this book I have giggled and laughed aloud, then just as quickly read on in horrified silence; certainly there is plenty of further reading to match your scatological threshold. In Roman times to snap your fingers – *concrepare digitos* – meant you needed the chamber-pot. Birds do it, bees do it, even intellectual fleas do it, so let's snap our fingers and enter the chamber.

1

THE HISTORY OF DUNG

Amendments are a bettering and improving of Earth, which improvement is made with all sorts of Dungs, according to the temper and employment of the Earth.

J. de la Quintinye The Compleat Gard'ner, *tr. John Evelyn* (1699)

Law and Ordure

Old English in derivation, dung is a four-letter word that is perfectly acceptable in polite circles, most people understanding its excretive rather than expletive qualities. Waste that should never knowingly be wasted, dung emerges, unlike its fellow passenger urine, from the digestive system potent and redolent with readily available compounds such as urea, uric acid, soluble phosphates and potash salts. Shakespeare hotly dismisses it with 'Out dunghill!', while elsewhere noting 'Our dungie earth alike Feeds Beast as Man'. More subtly, in *The Comedy of Errors*, Antipholus asks 'What is she?', to which Dromio replies: 'A very reverend body: ay, such a one, as a man may not speak of, without he say "Sir reverence".' Sirreverence ('save reverence') was an Elizabethan euphemism for dung.

Another Elizabethan slang word for human excrement and privy houses was jakes, which has filtered into current usage in the phrase 'to give someone a kick up the jacksie'. Jakes is how Shakespeare would have us pronounce Jacques in *As You Like It*, so that it sounds like a variant of japes – a device to amuse; this is another example of the playwright's use of dark humour to entertain his audience. So Elizabethan and Jacobean audiences could revel in the black-clothed melancholic gentleman in his 'inky cloak', adrift with his duke, trying to balance the enchanted, wild forest with cynical moralising and a courtly pose. Oppressed by responsibility, he was forced into action by the hand of fate. But what hope is there of gravitas and respect when your name means dung. Sir John Harington, godson of Queen Elizabeth, knew his readers would have been acquainted with Ovid's *Metamorphoses* and its cast of classical gods, goddesses and heroes, so what better title for his paper than 'The Metamorphosis of Ajax'. Just so the coiners of the cleaning product Ajax hoped to evoke an image of gleaming bathroom china.

The origin of one alternative term, manure, is neatly illustrated by Shakespeare when he juxtaposes manure with industry. The word manure is derived from the Latin manus ('hand'), and its roots are shared by such words as manoeuvre; all involve hands-on work, as described in Daniel Defoe's *Robinson Crusoe*: 'The land which I had manured or dug.' Although no longer in common parlance, the word 'manurance' means precisely what it says, but in the seventeenth century it enjoyed a wider definition as cultivation of the mind or faculties. Shakespeare's contemporary Francis Bacon, failed and forgotten as a courtier but remembered for his *Essays*, wrote about 'the culture and manurance of minds in youth', thus giving a whole new meaning to 'a fertile imagination'.

The powerful notions of origin, creation and generation are encompassed in that robust Greek word *genesis*. Genesis is also the first book of the Bible, and its first chapter recounts the symbolic creation in seven days of Heaven and Earth, the waters (but not rain), herbs and fruits, light and dark, fish and fowl, and, the day before man, beasts and creeping things. So the sacred scarab or dung beetle was already at work sanitising the Garden of Eden before Adam and Eve arrived. Sacred to the ancient Egyptians from the third millennium BC, dung beetles were associated in form and function with the solar deity Khepri and with ideas of spontaneous generation and the renewal of life. Large green stone scarabs, green possibly to represent the life dung gives to the soil, served as substitutes for the hearts of dead men, and were often inscribed with spell 30B in the Egyptian funerary literature commonly known as the Book of the Dead. An instantly recognisable shape formed in glazed steatite, faience or semi-precious stones, each was decorated underneath with designs, messages of good luck, charms or power statements. Inspired by one such exhibit in the British Museum, in the 1960s the London jeweller Richard Ogden created a scarab beetle ring crafted in Fabergé style out of molten gold, which was duly presented to Ringo Starr of the Beatles.

The worship and honouring of the dung beetle, technically a coprophage, remained sacred only in its name until in 1911 J. Henri Fabre published *The Life and Love of the Insect*, an inspiration to the young naturalist Gerald Durrell and an essential esoteric read. Rejoice in his introduction:

> the Dung-beetles, the dealers in ordure, the scavengers of the meadows contaminated by the herd. . . . What are our ugliness and beauty, our cleanliness and dirt to her? With refuse, she creates the flower; from a little manure, she extracts the blessed grain of the wheat. Notwithstanding their filthy trade, the Dung-beetles occupy a very respectable rank. Thanks to their usually imposing size; to their severe and irreproachably glossy garb; to their short, stout, thickset shape; to the quaint ornamentation either of their brow or, also, of their thorax, they cut an excellent figure in the collector's boxes, especially to our own species, oftenest of an ebony black, we add a few tropical species flashing with gleams of gold and ruddy copper.

Henri Fabre, aided by his father, his wife and his children, devoted his life to studying the habits of dung beetles in Provence, where flourish just a few of the over 7,000 species that cleanse the world.

In complete contrast to the nobility of the dung beetle's diligence is regal idleness. In ancient Greece King Augeas of Elis was the wealthiest man on earth in flocks and herds; by divine dispensation his livestock were immune to disease and fecund, never miscarrying and producing mostly female offspring. His pedigree herds included 300 white-legged black bulls, 200 red stud bulls and a magical 12 silvery-white bulls. Fertile and productive, the dung from Augeas' cattleyards and sheepfolds had overflowed across the neighbouring Peloponnese valley pastures to a depth that prevented ploughing. Hercules, for his fifth labour, offered to clear in one day the bovine stables, filled with dung that had accumulated over thirty years from some 3,000 cattle. Knowing it was impossible, Augeas promised Hercules a tenth of his prized cattle if he succeeded. Taking the advice of Menedemus the Elean, and with the help of Iolaus, Hercules breached the yard walls in two places and then diverted the rivers of Alpheus and Peneus so that their waters rushed together through the yards, sweeping away all the dung and cleansing the lower pastures. But lateral thinking won him no thanks, as Copreus the Herald (whose name, appropriately enough, translates as 'dung-man' – perhaps the original shit-stirrer?) raced to tell Augeas that Hercules had cheated. This news initiated further disputes. But the core of the story describes a tactic used down the centuries for flushing out problems and heroically depicted in the myriad magnificent statues of river gods in Roman, Renaissance, Mannerist and Baroque gardens.

The Farnese statue of Hercules resting after his labours (and its copies) positively litter grand gardens, whereas representations of Venus Cloacina are almost unknown. The Latin word *cluo* ('I cleanse') provides the root for both cloaca, a sewer or drain, and Cloacina, the cleanser. The pursuit of Greek culture and

THE

LIFE AND LOVE OF THE INSECT

BY
J. HENRI FABRE

TRANSLATED BY
ALEXANDER TEIXEIRA DE MATTOS

A. & C. BLACK, LTD.
4, 5 & 6 SOHO SQUARE, LONDON, W. 1.

The frontispiece to Henri Fabre's book on dung beetles, which so inspired the young Gerald Durrell. It is an esoteric read of poetic charm.

Virgil's lines that illustrate this scene – 'Easy is the way down to the Under-world: by night and by day dark Hades' door stands open; but to retrace one's steps and to make a way out to the upper air, that's the task, that is the labour' – echoes the experience of trawling the filth of the Cloaca Maxima or Great Sewer of Rome, or the Thames in London.

great works were the hall-marks of the fifth king of Rome, Tarquinius Priscus, whose finest achievements included the building of Rome's Cloaca Maxima ('Great Sewer') in the late sixth century BC. Some six hundred years later Pliny the Younger described the Emperor Trajan's decree that offenders who had served ten years of a sentence of hard labour could be transferred to cleaning the sewers.

Ancient Roman criminals were executed on the Gemonian steps and their bodies dragged away with hooks and thrown into the sewers. After his martyrdom St Sebastian's body was dragged to the Cloaca Maxima and thrown in, confirmation to onlookers that Christians were full of guilt and dishonour. Roman authorities condemned many Christians to build the baths of Diocletian in Rome, and centuries later their glorious edifice was consecrated by Pope Pius IV as the Church of Santa Maria degli Angeli. Victorians with a crude sense of humour bought chamber-pots dedicated to the goddess Cloacina and inscribed with:

> Oh Cloacina, Goddess of this place,
> Look on thy servant with a smiling face.
> Soft and cohesive let my offering flow –
> Not rudely swift, nor obstinately slow.

Foul Filth

The town of Cambridge encapsulates the inescapable history of urban stench. In 1267 Henry III, on his way with a large army to suppress the insurgent barons entrenched on the Isle of Ely, sought to instil domestic order in Cambridge:

> Moreover the king wills that the town of Cambridge be cleansed of dung and filth and be kept clean and the conduits be opened as of old they used to be, and be kept open, in order that filth may flow away through them, unless some other use or need stand in the way and that obstacles impeding their passage be removed and especially that the great ditch of the town be cleansed. For the observing of which things there shall be appointed two of the more lawful burgesses in every street, sworn before the mayor and bailiffs, the chancellor and masters being invited to this if they wish to be present.

In September 1386 a parliamentary session was held in Cambridge, after the king had personally sent word to the Chancellor to clean up the town before the royal retinue arrived. The Statute of Cambridge, which legislated for improved national sanitation, illustrated how low standards had fallen: 'so much dung and filth of the garbage and entrails, as well of beasts killed as of other corruption, be cast in ditches, rivers and other waters . . . the air is greatly corrupt and infect, and many maladies and other intolerable diseases do daily happen'.

Although dependent on one another, town and gown were in open conflict in Elizabethan Cambridge. A contemporary proverb captures their attitude: 'A Royston horse and a Cambridge intransigent Master of Arts are a couple of creatures that give way to nobody.' The former were the packhorses that carried malt to London, while the latter needs no explanation. By 1574 the streets of Cambridge were foul, plague was rife and the medieval King's Ditch skirting the town was little more than an open sewer. Dr Andrew Perne, then Vice-Chancellor of the University, and his enemy Mayor Roger Slegge were forced to overlook their differences in a bid to end odour and bring order to the town. Finally they agreed on eleven measures that would pertain for twenty years and, it was hoped, solve the problem. Five of the clauses related to dung:

1. All householders, inhabitants, scholars and churchwardens were to sweep and cleanse the streets on Wednesdays and Saturdays and have all the muck carted to the common dumps or into the fields by common carters. Innkeepers and horsekeepers were not allowed to dump manure in the streets, except just before removal time. Two overseers were appointed in each parish and they were to receive half of the fines imposed. The carters were to be paid by levying a special tax, to be assessed by a joint committee of two members of the university and two from the town.

3. No carts with iron-shod wheels were to be allowed in the town except when harvest-carting. The dung-carts were to have 'bare' wheels.

4. No pigs of any kind were to be allowed in the streets, college precincts or churchyards unless accompanied by a drover, on pain of a 4d fine. Runaway pigs would incur a fine of 4d on the drover.

5. No ducks or geese were to be allowed in the streets, on pain of 2d fine.

7. Nobody must throw the carcass of a dead animal – pig, cat, dog, rat, fowl, vermin or fish – into the streets, lanes or churchyards, or anywhere within a quarter-mile of the town, on pain of a 3s 4d fine; instead they must bury them on their own ground or 3 feet deep at the common dump. Dead horses and oxen were to be taken to the common dunghill, or further out of town. No corpses were to be thrown in the river. Parents and guardians would be held responsible for children offending in this respect.

At around this time Edmund Spenser published *The Faerie Queene*, his celebration of Queen Elizabeth, but William Cecil, Lord Burghley, refused to pay him for a 'song'. He might have been minded to rededicate the following lines: 'The dunghill kind Delights in filth and foul incontinence. . . .'

Later in Oxford the sharply critical antiquarian Anthony à Wood wrote disparagingly about Charles II and his court after their 1665 summer in Oxford: 'Though they were neat and gay in their apparell, yet they were very nasty and beastly, leaving at their departure their excrements in every corner, in chimneys, studies, colehouses, cellers. Rude, rough, whoremongers; vaine, empty, careless.' Nasty and beastly but surely not alone in their foul habits, as demonstrated all too vividly by Wood's contemporary Samuel Pepys, diarist and chronicler of his bowel movements:

> *11 October 1663:* . . . all day within doors, I finding myself neither to fart nor go to stool after one stool in the morning, the effect of the electuary last night. And the greatest of my pains I find come by my straining to get something out backwards, which strains my yard and cods, so as to put me in a great and long pain after it. . . . For all this, I eat with a very good stomach, and as much as I use to do. . . . After supper to bed as I use to be, in pain, without bringing wind and shitting. . . .
>
> *28 December 1664:* I waked in the morning about 6 o'clock and my wife not come to bed, I lacked a pot but there was none, and bitter cold, so was forced to rise and piss in the chimney, and to bed again.

Ten months later, when the court was in Oxford escaping the Great Plague and behaving incontinently, Pepys had also moved out to Mrs Clarke's at Greenwich:

> *28 September 1665:* And so to bed, and in the night was mightily troubled with a looseness (I suppose from some fresh damp linnen that I put on this night): and feeling for a chamber-pott, there was none, I having called the mayde up out of her bed, she had forgot I suppose to put one there: so I was forced in this strange house to rise and shit in the chimney twice; and so to bed and was very well again.

One assumes it was all cleared out with the ashes in the grate and stored for the nightmen, such as John Wigley, who effected removal at a 'reasonable rate'. In turn the waste was dumped into communal cesspits and open sewers which were regularly scavenged by the poorest of the poor (known as 'tossers') who hoped to find brass among the muck. After the Great Fire of London in 1666 both Christopher Wren and John Evelyn proposed a comprehensive redevelopment underground of the water supplies and sewage system, but it would be nearly 200 years before this was achieved.

Repositories of the Past

The midden is a treasure trove of evidence of lifestyle, diet and climate for archaeologists and researchers, and human middens in the Orkneys and in Mexico are described later in Chapters 2 and 7 respectively. A series of research papers have been published showing how animal middens can aid the understanding of climate and vegetation change over the last century. In South Africa J.S. Carrión, L. Scott, and J.C. Vogel have used the dung middens of the hyrax (small rabbit-like mammals also known as rock badgers) to monitor twentieth-century changes in montane vegetation of the Eastern Free State. Using palynology (pollen analysis), the chronological strata of the hyrax dung accumulations have shown the potential for long pollen sequences that mirror their foraging and behaviour. Their study site was in a predominantly grassland area around a rock shelter which they called Rooiberg Midden II.

Working with twentieth-century midden samples, the researchers used radiocarbon dating to provide accurate dates. The change of land use over the last century and environmental changes such as periods of drought and flood can all be tracked in the numerous pollen types, from pine, eucalyptus and buddleia to aquatics, ferns and fungal spores, as well as internal parasites, Trichuris and eggs from dung origin. Sites for pollen analysis are rare in Africa but the wide range of animal middens can yield information about the fossil environment. Once again species of hyrax are widespread but because of the arid conditions their midden accumulations of plant

In South Africa hyena middens have provided invaluable evidence of their diets – illustrating a cross-section of the local fauna – but the pollen contained in their faeces also serve as indicators of climate change.

material and faecal pellets are held together by dried urine. Coprolites, or fossil dung, have been studied from many species, such as the Dassie rats who live only in the Namib desert; brown hyena in southern Africa; and striped hyena in northern Africa and the Middle East. There are plans to study bat guano for pollen evidence.

Palynology was also used in the 1980s by O.K. Davis and R.S. Anderson to study packrat middens in the south-western States. In Owl Canyon, Colorado, they found no fewer than twenty-eight types of pollen. Overall they examined four types of midden material, including samples of packrat faecal pellets, in some fifty-four packrat middens. By comparison, the faecal pellets contained a greater proportion of pollen of zoophilous types than the midden samples. Some pollen probably arrived at the site through plant material brought in by the packrats. The scientists used the data they collated to examine fossil packrat midden samples, dating back to 14,000 BC, from sites at Owl Canyon in Colorado and the Organ Pipe Cactus National Monument in Arizona.

Similar research work has been carried out throughout the States. One further interesting study was conducted in Lamar Cave in Yellowstone National Park, where midden evidence enabled the scientists to compare the species and numbers of fauna that roamed the park from around 2,800 BC to the present day. As well as wood-rat dung, they found that of wolves, coyotes, hawks and owls. Finally faecal pellets can be used to compare the size of bushy-tailed woodrats from 11,000 BC and today's populations in Idaho and north-western Utah. The middens of stick-nest rats in caves and rock shelters have been studied in central Australia by S. Pearson to identify the pollen spectra over the last 3,000 years. Far from being a worthless excrescence, in this context dung may help Pearson to interpret ecological changes in this area over the period. The basic tendency of animals to live away from their excreta has created a testament of the environment that shaped their lifestyle and habits.

Degradation

Apart from the gross infliction of pain, further degradation with excreta illustrates man's capability and culpability for inhumanity. The ancient Persians condemned criminals to death by 'scaphis-mus' or boat (*scapha*) torture, used, according to Plutarch, for Mith-ridates's death in Artaxerxes. The condemned man is forced to lie in a boat, which is then covered by another boat of the same shape and size; only the man's head, hands and feet are exposed. The boat is turned so that it always faces the sun, to attract flies. The prisoner is force-fed, with milk and honey poured down his throat and over his face. As he starts to urinate and defecate, the ensuing corruption and putrefaction attract more flies, more maggots and more worms. His flesh and intestines rot in his own fly-blown excrement, as gradually, unremittingly, the body is eaten away. Mithridates took seventeen days to die. An alternative version, ordered by Parysatis for the slayer of her son Cyrus, was a scaphis-mus formed out of two ox-hides, in which the murderer took fourteen days to die.

Carl Gustav Jung had a very pious upbringing within the strict Lutheran faith, but his childhood was marred by a recurring shocking vision that haunted him. He saw God the Father, the Almighty, sitting on his golden throne in Heaven and 'dropping an enormous turd' on to a cathedral below. He awaited damnation but when it did not come he took it to mean that God was showing him what he actually was – the 'ego of the universe'. Was it an unconscious recollection of the Old Testament book of Nahum: 'Behold, I am against thee, saith the Lord of hosts; and I will discover thy skirts upon thy face, and I will show the nations thy nakedness, and the kingdoms thy shame. And I will cast abominable filth upon thee, make thee vile, and will set thee as a gazing-stock.' Perhaps it echoed Martin Luther's threat to stand in protest with his own turd around his neck? Jung later wrote: 'I was not

An illustration from *Victorian Comic Tales: Delightful People* – look at the title on the score.

aware at this time [before his vision] that the devil, properly speaking, had been born with Christianity.' Perhaps this was the precursor of the phrase used when things go seriously wrong, you 'have been shat on from a great height'.

A distant echo can be traced in Kipling's poignant poem 'Mesopotamia 1917', published in his postwar collection of 1919 entitled *The Years Between*:

> They shall not return to us, the resolute, the young,
> The eager and whole-hearted whom we gave:
> But the men who left them thriftly to die in their own dung,
> Shall they come with years and honour to the grave?

Six recriminative verses on the waste of life because of incompetent leaders are closed with:

> But the slothfulness that wasted and the arrogance that slew,
> Shall we leave it unabated in its place?

Political mudslinging has cleaned up considerably since Napoleon described Talleyrand as 'a pile of shit in a silk stocking'. Imagine the outrage in the newspapers if the following exchanges, recorded in *The Pearl* of July 1879, took place today. The 'rival toasts' were exchanged between Captain Balls of a Yankee frigate and an English man o'war: 'Here's to the glorious American flag: Stars to enlighten nations, and Stripes to flog them.' Quick was Jack's reply: 'Then here's to the ramping, roaring, British Lion, who shits on the stars, and wipes his arse on the stripes.' In 1929 a Congressman from Iowa and another from Maine took to using limericks to throw dirt at one another. The former's read:

> Here's to the State of Iowa
> Whose soil is soft and rich.
> We need no turd
> From your beautiful bird,
> You red-headed son of a bitch.

And in retort the Congressman from Maine answered:

> Here's to the American Eagle,
> That beautiful bird of prey:
> He flies from Maine to Mexico,
> And he shits on Iowa on the way.

America's 36th President Lyndon Baines Johnson was asked by a reporter why he had embraced Richard Nixon on the latter's return from a tour of South America. Johnson replied: 'Son, in politics you've got to learn that overnight chicken shit can turn to chicken salad.'

The purge and degradation of Jewish populations under Hitler's regime during the Second World War started as rhetoric and culminated in holocaust. Faced with certain extermination, many Jews hid in the excrement in latrines or sewers. In 1990 Robert Marshall compiled the memories of the survivors of the Lvov ghetto in Poland, and published them as *The Sewers of Lvov. The Last Sanctuary from the Holocaust*, an account of the bravery, endurance and generosity shown by these desperate people. Their story is almost beyond belief.

In the 1890s Italian engineers in the Polish town of Lvov had built an underground sewage system that was flushed by the River Peltwa; years later part of it ran under the Jewish ghetto that had been created in the 1940s. One of the chief sewer inspectors, who knew every inch of the underground channels, was a Catholic Pole named Leopold Socha, who had a wife and two small children. One day Socha discovered in the sewers Ignacy Chiger, who also had a wife and two small children, and Jacob Berestychi, and the two men confided that they were planning to use the channels as a hideout. With what money they had left they negotiated for Socha to provide food and water when the time came. On 31 May 1943 there was a final great clearance of the ghetto, and some 4–5,000 desperate Jews fled into the sewers along the escape route created by Chiger and Berestychi. The River Peltwa swept hundreds of them back through the sewer openings where they were shot like rats, while others stumbled along the service paths in search of refuge. On the first night about a hundred people sheltered in the cavern below the church of Our Lady of the Snows which adjoined the municipal lavatories: 'So here was their first home in the sewers: cold, wet and reeking of shit.'

Chiger and Berestychi made contact with Socha, who risked everything to bring food and drink to what he was expecting to be no more than ten or fourteen people. Water was rationed to half a cup a day, and dysentery and dehydration rapidly took hold. 'The walls of the cavern were constantly wet and crawled with a weird strain of albino insects. They were regularly invaded by small squadrons of rats, ferocious in their quest for food.'

The core group was finally reduced to just ten people, including the children, who lived in these appalling conditions from 1 June 1943 to 28 July 1944, emerging anaemic, emaciated and skeletally deformed. There were a few bright moments. One day, for example, Socha delivered a whole sack of potatoes, nonchalantly wheeling them along in full sight of the Germans. He had liberally powdered the potatoes with chalk, and asked everyone to stand back while he tipped the 'diseased' potatoes, apparently coated in lime for safety, straight down the inspection chamber of the sewers! Chiger and Berestychi were there to harvest them.

Familiar Faeces

The careful placing of dung in appointed middens, as markers or ready for use, is a feature of both man and beast. Badger setts are notoriously smelly, although in fact they mark only the edges of their territory by a system of small pits in which they defecate. Giant otters, which live in large family groups in the rivers of South America, manifest their territorial rights with a powerful odour. The whole group will select an area of riverbank, trample it down and defecate prodigiously – essentially creating a large family latrine. The flattened ground and the stench alert any other otters that this is their territory.

Otters are rarely seen, but they leave behind their spraints or droppings. In South America giant otters create a stinking latrine by the water's edge to mark their territory.

Thomas Hyll, who wrote for the modest Elizabethan gardener, quoted many classical sources when he argued for the right placing of dung:

> There were in ancient time, as Pliny recordeth, certain wittie Husbandmen, that wholly refused and forbad the dunging of Gardens placed nigh to the dwelling houses: in that this dunging might not onely infect the aire thereabout, but cause also the crescent things to prove both unsavorier and more corrupt. And in this matter the worthy writers of Husbandry commended highly the Greek Poet Hesiodus, which writing very cunningly of Husbandry, omitted the dunging of the fields, and Garden plots, contented rather to counsell unto healthfulnesse, then willed the same to fertility. Insomuch as it was supposed enough at that time, to have fatned the fields and Garden plots with the leaves and empty cods of Beanes, Peason, Tares, and such like, turned work-manly in with the earth in due season of the yeare.

Hyll's work also rapidly encouraged the use of dung and manurance.

In the mid-nineteenth century the Industrial Revolution reached its apogee in the 1851 Great Exhibition, a celebration of technology and the machine-made product. Running counter to this was the Arts and Crafts revival spearheaded by William Morris. Morris and his circle embraced the bounty of the earth and physical contact with the sensual pleasures of the soil, themes that pervade not only his designs but also his philosophy and lifestyle. Morris liked nothing better than harvesting and eating the produce from his gardens at the Red House and Kelmscott Manor. Curiously the most frequent mention of dung appears in his requests to his daughter May to raise worms on dung for his fishing expeditions.

When did man first observe that good dung makes for better green leaves? It was certainly long before scientists analysed and then synthesised nitrogen. Writing as early as 1933 A. Osborn compared the use of artificial fertilisers in the garden with people downing stimulants and tonics. He argued that manures offered texture and fermentation gases that lightened and fed the soil, and he reckoned cow, fowl and pig manure to be of greatest value, along with night soil (human excrement). The twenty-first century has dawned with the growth of organically produced meat, fish and vegetables, with recycled waste at the heart of the process. On the wild side, modern research is showing that the grazing and dunging cycle of indigenous herbivores in Kenya can sustain and maintain higher populations than introduced herds. The history of dung certainly has long roots – and offers the promise of exotic blooms to come.

2

ARCHITECTURAL MOVEMENTS

Every man is the architect of his own fortune.

Sixteenth-century proverb

Elegant Ornament

The need to house habitual and necessary bodily waste from humans and animals has led to many exotic constructions and unsightly windy hovels. At the luxurious end of the market, where better to start than a quote from *The Works of Architecture of Robert and James Adam, Esquires* (1778):

> Movement is defined as 'meant to express the rise and fall, the advance and recess, with other diversity of forms, in the different parts of a building, so as to add greatly to the picturesque of its composition. For the rising and falling, advancing and receding, with the convexity and concavity, and other forms of great parts, have the same effect in architecture, that hill and dale, foreground and distance, swelling and sinking have in a landscape: that is, they serve to produce an agreeable and diversified contour, that groups and contrasts like a picture and creates a variety of light and shade, which gives great spirit, beauty and effect to the composition. It is not always that such variety can be introduced into the design of any building, but where it can be attained without encroaching upon its useful purposes, it adds much to its merit as an object of beauty and grandeur.

Robert Adam reputedly designed more British buildings, inside and out, than any other architect. One obituary described his fertile genius in elegant ornament – a good subtitle for this section and expressive of the buildings associated with the gathering, distribution and disguise of dung in every form. At the cliff-top Culzean Castle in Ayrshire Adam demonstrated his fertile imagination by converting a fortified tower-house into a sham medieval castle complete with a Romano-Gothic viaduct, financed in part by the Home Farm. Four rectangular stables designed on a canted square plan are connected by four archways creating a square, with another four church-like buildings adorned with crosses and embattled gables ranged at right angles to it. This was an elaborate architectural disguise for the pursuit of mundane agricultural activities. While Adam's work took him south from Scotland, our journey takes us north, to the Orkney Islands off the coast of Caithness, where there are buildings spanning a period of time of more than five thousand years.

One of the earliest sites, on the mainland at Skara Brae in the Bay of Skaillon, was inhabited from about 3,100 to 2,500 BC. The best preserved Neolithic village in northern Europe, it was exposed to view by a wild storm in 1850. In life, as now, it was surrounded by pastureland and small fields of wheat and barley. Although coastal erosion has brought the site a little nearer to the water's edge, the buildings were always vital to protect the people from the wild westerly winds that sweep across the area. The people of an earlier village had carefully collected their every-day waste – including human and animal excrement – and piled it into large middens to decompose. Their buildings were free-standing, and are now almost entirely lost, probably because they lacked a good accumulation of midden material to protect them. Over the years the middens grew in size and were then redistributed into substantial mounds, inside which the people of Skara Brae built their houses, connected by subterranean passageways. Stone was plentiful, and was used to create dry-stone frontages and internal divisions, as well as to roof the passageways, which were then covered with midden soil. Researchers have long puzzled over why they used midden soil when there was so much stone available, but it seems that the midden fulfilled several

The Church of St Giles (in the background) was built in 1625 at the door of the French Church in Hog Lane, but by 1730 the accumulation of filth meant that the floor of the church was 8ft lower than its surrounds. Note the disgusting street drain, complete with dead cat. The woman at the window is throwing out her husband's mutton, not the contents of his chamber-pot. *The Four Times of the Day – Noon*, William Hogarth (1738)

functions. Its dense form was ideal for wind- and weather-proofing, while the subterranean passageways within it meant that the site had only one entrance, easily guarded against unwelcome visitors and stray animals. The individual dwellings (with identical internal layouts) were reached by sinuous passages cut through the midden, whose design threw the wind away from their doors. The midden bound the community together and fixed its boundaries, and may thus have been a physical symbol of a strong community spirit.

An Unclean Tower Harbours no Birds

The primary fertile and elegant architectural ornament has to be the dovecote. Initially the Romans kept pigeons and doves in the roof spaces of their houses and farm buildings, but later they developed exterior terracotta roof fittings for use in towns, and finally specially designed *columbaria*. Varro describes a white-painted circular tower structure with a conical roof, which maximised fresh meat and egg production and produced the finest agricultural fertiliser. Ovid confirms the need for cleanliness: 'You see how the doves come to a white dwelling [and] how an unclean tower harbours no birds.' Perhaps the modern small white dovecote on a post is a distant echo of this?

The roots and origins of Isfahan are documented on Babylonian cuneiform tablets from the first millennium BC. Ringed by rugged mountains, Isfahan lies on a plateau at a height of 1,590m midway between Tehran and Shiraz. In the fourteenth century the indefatigable traveller and writer Ibn Battutah (who Tim Mackintosh-Smith calculates covered some 79,000 miles) noted the magnificent pigeon towers that graced the views in and around the city. The large pigeon populations were housed in brick towers that were coated with lime and provided with hollow niches for nesting; copious amounts of dung were regularly collected and spread across the surrounding barren earth. In winter the floodwaters of the River Zayandeh

Jean Chardin was a jeweller and merchant who travelled extensively in Persia during the late seventeenth century. His *Voyages* noted that the dovecotes in Isfahan were 'six times bigger than the biggest in Europe'. Constructed of brick, they were plastered and coated all over with lime inside and out, and had hollowed niches for nesting.

Ruh were allowed to flood the fields, with any excess being stored in vast underground cisterns. The combined effect of the dung and the water transformed the desert into a Persian paradise, a fertile plain ringed by barren soil and the Zagros mountains. In addition dozens of small conical structures made of brick mud were placed in the surrounding fields for doves.

When Shah Abbas I moved his imperial capital from Qazvin to Isfahan in 1598 he set about rebuilding the city, adding glittering domes to the skyscape of pigeon towers. Throughout the seventeenth century Isfahan enjoyed the reputation of being the most beautiful city in the world, verdant and arboreal, and particularly noted for its melon fields; it was a city in which to do business. In 1618 Thomas Herbert accompanied Charles I's ambassador

Sir Dodmore Cotton to the city. He wrote: 'Gardens . . . for grandeur and fragour . . . such as no city in Asia outvies.' For centuries visitors have been intrigued by Isfahan and its pigeon towers, which are still an intriguing part of the city skyline.

In England only the lord of the manor could build a dovecote (known as 'doocots' in Scotland). The oldest surviving example, built in 1346, is at Garway in Herefordshire, while other surviving ones at Athelhampton House in Dorset and at East Harling in Norfolk had a nesting capacity of 1,000 birds. The plain circular and occasionally square towers belie the complex timber frameworks within. The birds flew in and out at the top, while the husbandman entered via a small door at the base, and used a complex moving ladder system to collect the eggs and squabs for the table. He also carried out any essential maintenance. The Normans introduced the beehive design that was most commonly used, as in the 1648 Rendall's Dovecote on the Orkney mainland. The sides of the building have four decorative stone shale ledges to stop rats running up the outside, and the pigeons enter through the hole in the roof. There is a low doorway at the base for human entry and collection, and there is an irregular arrangement of gaps in the stonework for nesting birds. On the nearby island of Shapinsay the Victorian owners of the medieval doocot at Balfour Castle converted it into a shower house.

In the late nineteenth century Gertrude Jekyll mourned the loss of dovecotes, which she described as admirable examples of fitness of purpose. She also explored their ornamental value by suggesting that the walled kitchen garden would be greatly enhanced by a four-gabled dovecote in one corner, with an apple room, a root store and a tea-house in the other three. This idea was partly taken up a hundred or so years later in The Alnwick Garden in Northumberland, where there are gabled dovecotes on the south-facing wall of the upper enclosure.

The love of utility and beauty in traditional arts and crafts, however, inspired many nineteenth-century architects to design functional ornaments. Charles Voysey viewed gardens as dream extensions of his buildings, dotted with summerhouses, seats and tables, gates, sundials, pigeoncotes and a bird bath. Equally, at Barncluith in Lanarkshire John James Joass designed a thatched dovecote that was more of a bird table than the egg, live larder and manure factory of its larger cousins. This trend was continued in the delightful modern blue and white hen house at West Green House in Hampshire, inspired by the famous willow pattern.

At Britwell Court in Burnham, Buckinghamshire, Waterhouse & Sons were called in by W. Christie-Miller to give the estate a 'general aggrandizement' between 1875 and 1896. Alfred Waterhouse's great masterpiece is the Natural History Museum in South Kensington, but he could equally provide a dramatic setting for one of its nature's subjects. Within Britwell's grounds he designed a magnificent clock tower and pigeon house – what the pigeons felt when the bell tolled we can only imagine, but it may have boosted dung production! Altogether the structure created a well-ordered empire in miniature, where the pigeons provided rich pickings for the gardens and the table alike, and the gardener could keep track of his working day against the backdrop of magnificent architecture and the sounds of cooing doves.

Hyll describes many sources of dung in *The Gardener's Labyrinth* but does not include rabbits, a major source of winter food in the sixteenth century when landowners employed warreners to ensure a plentiful supply. Hungry rabbits cannot get enough nourishment from their chosen leaves and roots in winter, so they have evolved a cunning plan. After eating they go into their burrows to defecate and then eat the still-warm faeces so that their digestive juices can extract any leftover goodness. Second time round the rabbits use communal mounds for their droppings, which provide a bunny bulletin board. Restoration of the formal Dutch-style gardens at Westbury Court in Gloucestershire, a style popularised by William and Mary, has gone so far as to include a re-creation of the seventeenth-century warren. Rabbits and immaculate gardens are rarely a happy combination but the warren's original purpose was to provide winter meat – will the re-creation go that far?

Dung or no dung this landscape is enhanced by the (guinea) piggy palace and pheasantry adorned with iron featherwork. This photograph appeared in 'Modern Gardens British and Foreign' (1926), edited by Percy Cane, who wrote that although traces of Art Nouveau remained in some German gardens, Herr Berthold Körting's garden showed broader and more intelligible modern work.

Modernist Manure

Garden designer Percy Cane wrote the text for a special winter number of *The Studio* magazine in 1926/7, entitled 'Modern Gardens British and Foreign'. Foreign in this case included America, France, Germany, Austria, Italy, Sweden, Denmark and Japan. In its array of black and white photographs, and a few coloured plates by Beatrice Parsons, dung, dunghills and compost heaps are conspicuous by their absence. But, joy of joys, there are two photographs of Berlin-based architect Herr Berthold Körting's own garden. One shows a low seven-course brick enclosure with a rocky slope rising behind it; the enclosure sports a white-painted plastered arch decorated with palm motifs and punctuated by two doors, each with two steps. Lined up behind the arch an elegant iron aviary soars upwards, with a matching metal palm motif at its centre. The former is a guinea-pig house and enclosure, the latter a pheasant pen. Another part of the garden is Japanese-inspired, with a stone lantern and a nine-storey dovecote rising like a pagoda, in true oriental fashion.

These two elements of Körting's garden embody a twentieth-century interpretation of Adam's definition of architectural movement in the creation of the picturesque, quoted at the beginning of this chapter. The cloudy fluttering of the doves, the kaleidoscopic colours of the pheasants and the miniature furry grazing of the guinea pigs are punctuated by the restful sounds of cooing, clucking, squeaking and purring.

Aviaries

The writings of Henry Wotton, who served twice as ambassador to Venice (for James I from 1604 to 1612 and for Charles I from 1621 to 1624), explore how irregularities in the garden can lead to delight and surprise. He observed how steep slopes and cunning devices contrasted with the symmetry of mannerist garden design. On his return from Venice he published *The Elements of Architecture*, in which he explored the artifice and conceits that so inspired him. He was particularly taken with aviaries and produced the following poetic description:

> In Aviaries of wire, to keepe Birdes of all sorts, the Italians (though no wastfull Nation) doe in some places bestow vast expence; including great scope of ground, varietie of bushes, trees of good height, running waters, and sometimes a Stove annexed, to contemper the Aire in Winter. So as those Chanteresses, unlesse they be such as perhaps delight as much in their wing, as in their voice, may live long, among so good provisions and roome, before they know that they are prisoners, reducing often to my memory, that conceit of the Romane

Herr Berthold Körting's garden was highly praised by Percy Cane as being 'interesting in its formality and suggestion of Japanese influence'. The pagoda is actually a dovecote!

Stoicke, who in comparison of his owne free contemplations, did thinke divers great and splendent fortunes of his time, little more than commodious captivities.

After the death of Charles I in January 1649, a survey of the manor of 'Wymbledon, alias Wimbleton' was carried out for his widow Henrietta Maria. The descriptions of the extensive gardens include many knots, a maze, an Oringe (sic) Garden (whose trees were valued at £240 with one lemon tree at £20), vineyards and a Hartichoke (sic) Garden extending to 44 perches of land. One can assume that all these required liberal dressings of manure, possibly supplemented by the Pheasant Garden. The visual imagery of brightly plumed birds is pleasing and their architectural domain reads very elegantly. Within an acre of land planted with deciduous and fruit trees and subdivided by lattices, and approached by a descent of twenty-three steps of stone, stood the six-roomed

Pheasant House, boarded within and without under a tiled roof. In addition there was a shed for the pheasant keeper, with four rooms and a tiled roof.

Ornamental birds were also kept confined at Wimbledon in a vast birdcage with three open turrets, 'very well wrought for the sitting and perching of birds'. At the centre of the cage was a fountain made of three lead cisterns, into which gilded lead pipes splashed pleasantly and pleasingly. A black and white marble pavement extended 104ft from the adjoining Balcony Room into the birdcage as a railed walk.

Privily

Animals seem better organised than humans, rarely soiling their homes and often creating an area dedicated to defecation. The golden mole from southern Africa is a good example. Easy prey for passing raptors and jackals, the moles have devised a series of subterranean chambers, one of which is well removed and dedicated to defecation. The removal of human waste by odourless means eluded many cultivated and sophisticated societies. Poorer medieval citizens were requested to squat a bow's shot away from any dwelling – from which practice derived the siting of the privy house.

Smoking disguises most smells, but could equally be a giveaway.

Today, as gardens diminish, houses are growing apace on modern developments, where en-suite facilities for every bedroom are regarded as a necessity. A century ago Edwin Lutyens's splendid architectural conversion of Lindisfarne Castle for Edward Hudson created a Vermeer-meets-Morris interior with nine bedrooms but only one bathroom. By comparison the thick walls of medieval Bodiam Castle disguised the discharges from some twenty garderobes into the moat. The architecture of Lindisfarne Priory has been described as Little Durham in layout, but a few of the Durham Dorter (dormitory) facilities would also have been convenient. It is described, with a novel approach to spelling, in Nathaniel Lloyd's excellent *A History of the English House* (1931):

Also there was a faire large house and a most decent place adioyninge to the west syd of the said Dortre, towards ye water for ye mounckes and nouices to resort vnto, called the prvies wch. was maide with two greate pillers of stone that did beare vp the whole floore thereof and every seate and pticiõ was of wainscott close of either syde verie

The latrines at Fountains Abbey in Yorkshire offered privacy and cleanliness. The bridge on the left leads over the diverted River Skell, which flushes all before it.

33

decent so that one of them could not see one another, when they weare in that place, there was as many seates of prvies on either syde as there is little wyndowes in ye wall, wch. wyndowes was to give leighte to every one of the saide seats wch. afterward was walled up . . . over ye saide seates is an other faire glasse wyndowe.

A similar layout can be discerned in the latrines of ruined Fountains Abbey near Ripon in Yorkshire.

Piety and strict living in the service of God were the tenets of the Carthusian monastic orders, their monks living as hermits in individual cells. The layout of cells is first recorded following the rebuilding of the Grande Chartreuse in the mountains of Dauphiné, Haute Savoie, France, after it was destroyed by an avalanche in 1132. The last English Charterhouse was founded at Mount Grace Priory in 1398, with fifty-two two-storey cells clustered around the great cloister; a stone water tower at the cloister's centre provided fresh water to each cell. After the Reformation the priory was sold in 1540, along with its home farm. Sadly over the next 350 years the buildings were slowly allowed to fall down, until they came into the hands of an Arts and Crafts enthusiast, Sir Lowthian Bell. Bell rebuilt Monk's Cell 8, and recently English Heritage restored his work as well as furnishing the cell and creating a garden. Today's visitor can follow the covered walk to an outer room with a wooden-seated privy, whose outlet goes straight down the outer wall, cleansed by water channelled from the pyramidal Spring House in the hillside. Today's cell seems a very pleasant escape from the world and far distant from the Carthusians' other liquid legacy – Chartreuse.

In Kirkwall, the capital of the Orkney Islands, a bishop's and an earl's palace lie alongside the magnificent medieval cathedral of St Magnus. In 1550 Bishop Reid improved his palace, equipping his own private chamber on the first floor with en-suite latrine and fireplace – sensible thinking for the cold, blustery climate. Robert Stewart (Mary Queen of Scots' illegitimate half-brother) and his son Patrick were renowned and feared as the tyrannical Earls of Orkney. Today the majestic Renaissance ruins of their

The Spring House at Mount Grace Priory near Northallerton in Yorkshire channels water around the outside of the monastery to wash away the outpourings from the individual monks' privies on to the fields below.

Discernible among the ruins of Mount Grace Priory are the enclosures for the individual monks' cells, each with an outside privy that was flushed down into the pastures below.

palace belie the misery involved in its creation. The chamber suites were lit by oriel windows, while the inner chamber had two further windows and was heated by a fireplace. It also boasted a well-placed latrine, offering privacy and a deal of comfort.

Privy shafts were created within the walls of castles and fortified manors but even if the drainage system was efficient (often straight into the moat) the walls of the shaft needed regular flushing. Sir William Petre's plans for the drainage system installed at Ingatestone Hall, Essex, in 1565 still exist. He had five stool-houses, each with a close-stool, next to the 'orte yarde', which was serviced by an elaborate system of water-pipes and drains. He brought a supply of 'very clear and sweet water' into every office in the house and then, by means of 'divers vaults and gutters of brick, very large, under ground, round about the whole situation of the house', flushed every office and drained the waters away.

Rainwater was collected via roof drains, succinctly described in the later Longford Manuscript (1678): 'Nay, art here hath so well traced Nature in the most ignoble conveyances (which are no less needful than the most visible conveniences) as to furnish every storey with private conduits for the suillage of the house, which are washed by every shower that falls from the gutters, and so hath vent from the very foundations to the top for the discharge of noisome vapours.' Around 1800 another Longford property in Ireland, Pakenham Hall Castle, was gothicised and castellated for Thomas Pakenham by Francis Johnson. Round towers were added on each corner, and a further almost detached four-storey tower was erected. This tower was dedicated to water-closets: there was a luxurious single one on the ground floor, while the basement and the first, second, third and fourth floors all had single but paired cubicles flushed via a rainwater tank at the top of the tower. Sixty years later further modifications were devised by Dublin architect J. Rawson Carroll: the flagstaff tower was adapted to hold a large water tank, supplemented by others across the roofscape; the lavatories were reduced to three that could be flushed properly; and the effluent was used to fertilise the fields at the bottom of the hill.

There is a pleasant sense of mixed metaphors in the diaper patterning of the elegant slender brick gabled towers that form the east front at Beckley Park near Oxford. Two of the three were built as privy towers, with privies on the top gabled floor connected by shafts to a water channel threaded beneath them. Beckley and its privies provided the model for Chrome in Aldous Huxley's *Chrome Yellow*. There were privy shafts in the Old Hall at Hardwick but when the Countess of Shrewsbury – better known as Bess of Hardwick – built her new prodigy house of 'more glass than wall', she and her guests were supplied with close-stools. The Hardwick Hall inventories of 1601 describe Bess's one as 'covered with blue cloth stitched with white, with red and black silk fringe'.

One of the ways to get on in society was to use the correct terminology, what Nancy Mitford termed U and Non-U. To utter the word toilet marked you as an outcast, while lavatory placed you comfortably on the social ladder. This was delightfully summarised in a Betjemanesque rhyme by Margaret Jenkins:

> Hubby sits on Auntie's toilet,
> smokes a handrolled cigarette.
> What a caper, no more paper.
> Pass us, ducks, the serviette.

However, the 'lavatorium' was where you washed your hands. The Augustinian priory of Newstead Abbey in Nottinghamshire had a lead lavatorium in its south cloister walk for the monks, and such was the efficiency of the water supply that the Byron family continued using it for three hundred years until Lord Byron sold the abbey in 1817.

A Withdrawing Room

Lodgings with en-suite facilities for the upper and middle classes become noticeably more fashionable from the fourteenth century. In 1343 the innovative work at the royal manor of Easthampstead in Berkshire was documented. The six large chambers in the buildings on either side of the gate in the courtyard were converted into thirteen small chambers served by new stairs, windows and oriels, and each with its own privy. Euphemisms abound for the medieval privy, privy house or privy chamber, including garderobe, withdraught, jakes, latrine, jericho, necessary and gong. Garderobe was the Norman-French term for a wardrobe (literally a dress store), which was not a piece of furniture but a room with a fireplace where the yeoman of the wardrobe and his assistants could repair clothes and hangings. There is a delightful example at Dunrobin in Sutherland. As the privy usually consisted of a small cell in which a pierced seat was placed over a shaft, you can understand the terms withdraught and gong, although 'withdraught' also meant a small room off a larger one.

Today we associate the privy chamber with high office, but its origins appear to lie in the room between the medieval king's bed-chamber (which also acted as his audience room) and his privy, which was in charge of the groom of the stool – in both senses. As medieval kingship evolved into Renaissance royal intrigue and mystery, the bed was moved first into a further, more private chamber and then into a suite beyond the private dining- and reception rooms. From the eighteenth century the groom of the stool was also transformed from a necessary cleaner to one of the most powerful and confidential royal servants. When Horace Walpole, for example, was staying at Woburn Abbey, he overhead a guest who had dropped a silver piece remark, 'Oh, never mind; let the Groom of the Chambers have it.' He was rapidly rebuked by the Duchess of Bedford with the comment, 'Let the carpet-sweeper have it; the Groom of the Chambers never takes anything but gold.'

It is said that Elizabeth I's Lord Treasurer, William Cecil, 1st Baron Burghley, built prodigiously as a form of relaxation, notably Burghley House, Theobalds and Cecil House in London. One of his privy towers at Burghley House remains as an en-suite facility to the brown drawing-room. Cecil House enjoyed a riverside position spanning the modern-day Strand and the River Thames, and in 1560 Sir Nicholas Bacon wrote to Cecil: 'Me thynkes ye prvye in ye west end ys ye lest and to nere ye logyng, to nere an hoven and to nere a lytle lardre. I thynk you had been better to have offendyd yor eye owtward than yor nose inward'!

The Grande Levee in the court of Louis XIV was attended by a chosen few to hear a detailed report on the healthy or otherwise appearance of the king's bowel movement. Versailles was equipped with no fewer than 264 'stools', 208 of which were covered with an array of luxurious fabrics. The other 56 were concealed by drawers or covers. Another design looked like a pile of books, which gave the craftsman some scope for a bit of fun, entitling the books *Voyages au Pays Bas* volumes I to IV and *Mystères de Paris*. The courts around which Versailles Palace was built also contained privies that were much used. Louis XIV only travelled by coach with ladies as he did not wish to be asked about questions of state, but as he did not agree with convenience stops he forbade his passengers this comfort while they were in his company.

'Gardy-loo' (from *gardez l'eau* – or watch out for the splash!) was hollered once a day from as high as ten storeys in pre-main drains

Edinburgh, as the accumulated contents of the close-stool were disgorged into the streets. With a touch of irony the Presbyterians insisted that the City Guard did not clean the streets on the Sabbath, giving an unusual take on the phrase 'odour of sanctity'. In *The Expedition of Humphrey Clinker* (1770), Tobias Smollett's character Win Jenkins reports on the city:

> We have got to Haddinborrough, among the Scots, who are civil enuff for our money, tho I don't speak their lingo. But they should not go for to impose upon foreigners; for the bills in their houses say, they have different easements to let; and behold there is nurro geaks in the whole kingdom, nor anything for poor sarvants, but a barrel with a pair of tongs thrown a-cross; and all the chairs in the family are emptied into this here barrel once a day; and at ten o'clock at night the whole cargo is flung out of a back windore that looks into some street or lane.

Win Jenkins was a near-contemporary of Samuel Johnson, who famously toured Scotland with James Boswell, observing succinctly that the Scots looked after one end of a man but not the other.

Flushed with Pride

In 1596 Queen Elizabeth's godson Sir John Harington published *The Metamorphosis of Ajax; a Cloacinean Satire*, which included a description of his great invention, the water-closet. He built one at his seat at Kelston near Bath and his godmother loyally installed one at Richmond Palace. Sir John assured his readers that if frequently used and flushed it would remain sweet, but if water was scarce just once after the twentieth user would suffice. To prevent over-enthusiastic flushing, he devised a scallop shell cover that disguised the sluicing mechanism.

Several reasons are cited for the lack of excitement for Harington's water-closet, first the lack of closing (odour-sealing) valves and secondly the invention of the back staircase. The French were the first to design the back or service staircase in the sixteenth century, and in the late seventeenth century Roger Pratt recorded the principles behind such a device, based on his experience at Coleshill. It was, he said, 'so contrived . . . that the ordinary servants may never publicly appear in passing to and from for their occasions there'. If you had staff who 'miraculously' removed the contents of your close-stool and, until the eighteenth century, often shared their living-space with it, there was little incentive for introducing complicated plumbing systems into the house. However, there were critical voices. Dean Jonathan Swift, generally known as the author of *Gulliver's Travels*, also wrote *Human Ordure*, a book about sewage, and in 1745 a pamphlet entitled *Directions to Servants*. In *Directions* he wrote:

> I am very much offended with those Ladies, who are so proud and lazy, that they will not be at the Pains of stepping into the Garden to pluck a rose, but keep an odious Implement, sometimes in the Bedchamber itself, or at least in a dark Closet adjoining, which they make Use of to ease their worst Necessities; and, you are the usual Carriers away of the Pan, which maketh not only the Chamber, but even their Cloaths offensive, to all who come near.

Some eighteenth-century houses, such as Kinross in Scotland and Easton Neston in Northamptonshire, incorporated 'service' mezzanines of small suites of rooms comprising a private closet or study, a servant's room and a close-stool room.

Celia Fiennes, who made a series of journeys around England between 1682 and 1712, was the daughter of a Cromwellian nonconformist and thus took great delight in useful arts. Water and its uses in houses and gardens were carefully noted in her journals, and on one trip to Windsor she observed: 'In the Castle yard is a little box the Queen has bought of Lord Godolphins (the garden joyns to the Duke of St Albans) for a little retreat.' She goes on to describe the rooms until she reaches 'the next was what was Prince George's dressing-roome . . . a closet that leads to a little place with a seate of easement of marble with sluces of water to wash all down; there is a back doore in the dressin roome to a little anty roome . . .'. At Chatsworth she found 'a batheing roome, the walls all with blew and white marble', but she appears not to have seen any of the newly installed water-closets with brass fittings and cedar woodwork (and with marble bowls for the duke and duchess and local alabaster for the remainder). The Duke of Chandos was so proud of his marble water-closet complete with 'plug cock and handles' that he had it installed unscreened in the corridor outside his library at Cannons.

Water Baby

In 1728 an unknown benefactor, reputedly Lord Burlington, saw a sickly apprentice chimney-sweep drawing an elevation of Whitehall's banqueting house on its ground-floor wall. Struck by the boy's precocious talent, he bought out his apprenticeship, paid for his education, sent him to Italy and supported him until he became a fully fledged architect. Isaac Ware fulfilled his early promise and wrote copious amounts on architecture with the zeal of a convert. His attention to every detail included wise words on drainage channels to cess pools and 'bog houses'. In his *A Complete Body of Architecture* (1756) he included a house plan with drain runs, recommending brick drains and sewers shaped like inverted arches such as could be found at the new Horse Guards building. Plans of sewers and drains for another large mansion depicted 'bog houses, a public sewer under the street and cesspits all without the building'. His humble origins were presumably long forgotten when he advised lodging servants over hen houses to avert common thievery of poultry.

The pan closet was developed by William Hawkins of Fleet Street. This device simply 'flushed' into a further chamber out of sight (but not out of smell). Stevens Hellyer, a cutting-edge plumber, bemoaned their popularity as late as 1891 in the tones of a tragic hero:

The light of a candle does not die down all at once. Often in its last flickering moments it extends its flame with so much vigour that a stranger to its ways may be pardoned for thinking that it had recovered its lost energy, and was coming back to life and light again. And so it is with the pan closet.

Water-closets were revolutionised by Joseph Bramah's invention of an efficient system with an effective valve, which he patented in 1778. By 1797 Bramah claimed to have sold over 6,000 systems and his firm continued making them until 1890. Although Pakenham Hall in Ireland relied on rainwater until 1875, a four-storey tower for water-closets was added to the rear of the house around 1800, where a rainwater cistern serviced one single-seater and three two-seater water-closets. The only rival was the fire-clay Hopper Closet, offered as the Long or the Short. The former was a conical pan flushed by a thin spiral jet of water. Self-appointed judge and author of both *The Plumber and Sanitary Houses* (1871) and *Principles and Practice of Plumbing* (1891), Mr Stevens Hellyer commented that the jet of water moved 'with such a twirling motion, that by the time it has twirled itself down to the trap it has no energy left to carry anything with it'. When they reached their sell-by date it was suggested they should be retained as rhubarb-forcers, with the dung piled up the outside rather than filling the interior!

Mr T.W. Twyford introduced an all-earthenware Washout Closet, using just an inch or two of water which 'gravitates through the trap in a most unselfish kind of way taking little or nothing with it', as Mr Hellyer delicately put it. The problems of flushing power, smell and noise were solved by Hellyer's own 'Optimus' Improved Valve Closet of 1870, with customers able to choose between a variety of casings, either mahogany or an elegant wickerwork chair.

We will celebrate Thomas Crapper as well as Joseph Bazalgette's stupendous sewage systems that ensured the health and welfare of London in the section entitled 'Convenient Waste', but we must mention here one Bazalgette exit that is of architectural merit. His system of sewers culminated at the Abbey Mills pumping station, which lifted low-level sewage 32ft to the outfall sewer. The station's exotic oriental design was certainly impressive – but was so instantly recognisable that it provided a navigational aid for the Luftwaffe in the Second World War.

Necessarily

In Virginia the College of William and Mary, founded in 1695, declared that the colonial centres of Jamestown and Yorktown would be superseded from 1699 by a new capital – Williamsburg. The ensuing creation of broad straight thoroughfares and imposing public buildings leading to smart town-houses surrounded by elegant pleasure gardens in Middle Plantation endorsed a new beginning, in a reign that lasted just under a century. Its state of rural dilapidation was halted in 1926 when restoration was started, and Colonial Williamsburg now extends over 175 acres with 88 original structures. Privies and 'necessary houses' were some of the essential outbuildings that have been carefully restored. Three of the grandest can be found in the grounds of the Governor's Palace – which were probably not used one night in July 1758 when Governor Fauquier noted that hailstones 1½in long and ¾in wide (3.8cm by 1.9cm) had broken every pane of glass on the north side and destroyed the gardens. On warm evenings dinner guests passed through the elegant double-doors that led from the supper room into the formal and fragrant ballroom garden, which was ornamented at its far corners with two elegant brick pavilions, sash-windowed and tiled, that were actually necessary houses. The contents were collected from without and distributed on to the gardens. To the west, after dallying in the maze and admiring the espaliered apples and clumped figs, guests found a further brick necessary house in the corner of the kitchen garden, strategically placed to assist visitors caught short or wishing to contribute to the garden's fertility.

The houses, gardens and estates of American President George Washington at Mount Vernon are carefully preserved as a

Virgil recommended planting trees in squares (quadrum) or staggered rows (quincunx), a system still used today. Thomas Rivers, doyen of fruit growers, advised forking in 30 to 40 tons of manure per acre to a depth of 20in when planting an orchard on poor soil.

Quadrum.

Quincunx.

Vox *quadret* **proprie notat priorem figuram ;** **metaphorice vero fecundam. Ita Cicero, de**

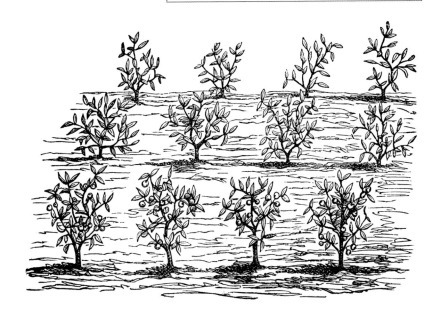

testament to philanthropic organisation. Washington wrote to William Pearce on 5 June 1796: 'Tell the Gardener I shall expect everything that a Garden ought to produce, in the most ample manner.' The upper and lower kitchen gardens that flank the house are matching rectangles which curve away into a point closed by a brick and tile tool house. Under the shade of some trees a small white-painted brick octagonal pavilion with sash windows is approached by two steps at the corner of the lower garden wall nearest the house. The door opens into a necessary house, with an earth tray positioned under the seat. On the kitchen garden side a trapdoor enables the tray to be removed and the contents put to good use.

At the Avoncroft Museum of Historic Buildings at Bromsgrove in Worcestershire is a reconstructed Georgian brick privy with earth closet, which originally stood in the grounds of Townsend House, Leominster. It looks to all intents and purposes like a garden pavilion, except that the lower sections of the sash windows are modestly panelled rather than glazed. Push open the door and you find a polished bench with no fewer than three holes, two large and one small, each with an individual lid. A deep cesspit was dug beneath, and as the pit filled up it was sealed with earth and ashes; once full, one hopes in the winter, the major task of emptying it was undertaken by a nightsoil man, who carried away the spoil in his 'lavender' cart or poured it on to the vegetable ground.

Roger Kilroy's lavatorial miscellany, *The Compleat Loo*, includes photographs of a six-seater privy at Chilthorne Dormer in Somerset and a one-and-a-half seater privy for a mother and child in a churchyard at Selling in Kent. A three-seater privy of Arts and Crafts perfection is tucked away in the garden of Kelmscott Manor in Oxfordshire. Embodying the Arts and Crafts philosophy of beauty and utility, it can also boast visits from William Morris, Dante Gabriel Rossetti et al.

Not beautiful but starkly useful was the 'netty' in Geordie outhouses, which combined the coalhouse and earth closet; it was 'flushed' using the ash and then stored the sewage for collection. Most commonly built in County Durham behind miners' terraced houses, each outhouse had two full-sized and two small doors, the larger doors giving access to the coal and the netty. There was a wooden seat over the earth, and waste was 'flushed' with ash which was deposited through the upper small door and then released at will. The lower small door provided access to shovel out the nightsoil, ready mixed as compost! Water-closets remained a privilege of the rich, the urban and the newly housed well into the twentieth century, and although earth closets might have been updated to high-level flushers, they remained outdoors.

Dung was not necessarily a bowshot or short trot away. In some cases it could form an integral part of the home. Cottages and dwellings were traditionally built using a timber frame infilled with wattle and daub or later in many cases with brick. Wattles were fashioned out of hazel rods which were sprung into place – rather like today's artisan wattle fences – and then plastered with daub. Daub was made by pounding a mixture of clay, straw and water, with the pounding often being performed by an animal 'walking' the mixture together. One of the best daubs was clay and straw mixed with cow dung, which dried hard. The daub was scratched while still wet to give a key to the later finer plaster. Finer but still coarse, a humble and primitive contrast to dwellings of the better sort. Alexander Pope, in *Of the Use of Riches*, conjured up the final moments of the once-mighty Duke of Buckingham, the 'lord of useless thousands ends', in the words: 'In the worst inn's worst room with mat half-hung, The floors of plaister, and the walls of dung.'

Well Wiped

Lord Chesterfield was determined to advise his son how to value time and use it well:

> I know a gentleman, who was so good a manager of his time, that he would not even lose that small portion of it which the calls of nature obliged him to pass in the necessary house, but gradually went

through all the Latin poets in those moments. He bought, for example, a common edition of Horace, of which he tore off gradually a couple of pages, carried them with him to that necessary place, read them first and then sent them down as a sacrifice to Cloacina; that was so much time fairly gained, and I recommend you to follow his example . . . it will make any book which you shall read in that manner very present in your mind.

Or to put it another way:

> There was a young fellow named Chivy
> Who, whenever he went to the privy,
> First solaced his mind,
> And then wiped his behind,
> With some well-chosen pages of Livy.

There are forty-one references in the Bible to the fig. Dried or fresh it has exceptional nutritional value and is highly esteemed as a safe laxative. The Romans introduced the fig tree into England along with the *triclinium* or outdoor dining-room. Figs were planted nearby not just for their luscious fruit but as a handy wipe; beautifully apt is Gertrude Jekyll's description: 'To pass the hand among the leaves of the Fig-tree, noting that they are a little harsh upon the upper surface and yet soft beneath.' Recycled paper sewn or nailed to the privy walls gave rise to my grandmother's joke: 'Dear Sir, Your letter that was before me is now behind me. Yours faithfully . . .' Postwar Britain may have continued to recycle paper in its remaining privies but indoor facilities for the masses were further revolutionised by the arrival of soft lavatory paper, which was no good for musical combs but luxurious to use.

Before the Second World War life for Harvey Ladew was perfectly delightful. An American with large private means, he energetically pursued his pleasures, and what an eclectic range they encompassed. Travel and languages fascinated him, and he read widely in French and Italian; passionate about riding, he explored Arabia and was friends with T.E. Lawrence and went hunting with the smartest English sets, the Quorn, Cottesmore and Belvoir. A good friend of his, interior designer Billy Baldwin, stated that Ladew was 'practically a lunatic on the subject of anything having to do with England'. In 1929 he purchased Pleasant Valley in Maryland, where he gave full rein to his artistic and designer tastes, to the extent that his outstanding gardens sported a full hunt in topiary. One imported idea, not shared with much enthusiasm by his friends, was English lavatory paper, despite the pleas of decorator Ruby Ross Wood that he should at least address the feelings of his guests and buy nice soft American toilet paper.

Part Two

THE PRODUCTS

Soil will not fail you

"Tom, away; mark the high noises."—*King Lear.*

Well-rotted manure mixed with potting compost makes a rich friable soil for container
plants. The problem of soft soil attracting cats
was certainly known to Victorian gardeners, as
depicted in this illustration from Shirley
Hibberd's *The Amateur's Greenhouse*.

INTRODUCTION

A writer . . . must know that dung-heaps play a very reasonable part in a landscape . . .

Anton Chekhov

In the sixth edition of his *Dictionary* (1785) Samuel Johnson defined the noun dung as 'the excrements of animals used to fatten ground'. For the verb he quoted Bacon's *Natural History*: 'It was received of old, that dunging of grounds when the west wind bloweth, and in the decrease of the moon, doth greatly help.' Guy Barter, writing in the March 2005 edition of *The Garden*, opened his profile of 'Soils and plant nutrition' with the heading 'Happy plants are healthier'.

The 'products' are what makes them happy, away from the horticultural equivalent of white sliced bread to wholemeal loaves; manures and composts kneaded into the soil slowly release nitrogen to feed plants as well as improving the soil structure and increasing its capacity to retain moisture. Humus-rich soil teams up with microbial activity to reduce plant pathogens and stop the soil suffering from 'tiredness'.

Just as wholemeal bread tastes better when coated with poppy seeds and grains, so a mulch of manure increases the fecundity of earthworms and other organisms, whose increased activity improves the permeability of the soil to water and air. Plant roots need to delve with ease so that they can draw nutrients in soluble form through their root hairs by osmosis; the more fine hairs the healthier the plants.

There is a crucial balance of nutrients: nitrogen for soft, leafy growth, phosphorus for good root growth and potassium – the word. *Swift.*

DUNG. *n. f.* [ᵭmeᵹ, Saxon.] The excrement of animals ufed to fatten ground.

For *dung*, all excrements are the refufe and putrefactions of nourifhment. *Bacon's Nat. Hiftory.*

I judge the likelieft way to be the perforation of the body of the tree in feveral places, one above the other; and the filling of the holes with *dung*, mingled with the medicine; and the watering of thofe lumps of *dung* with fquirts of an infufion of the medicine in dunged water, once in three or four days. *Bacon's Natural Hiftory.*

For when from herbs the pure part muft be won
From grofs by 'ftilling, this is better done
By defpis'd *dung* than by the fire or fun. *Donne.*

He foon would learn to think like me,
And blefs his ravifh'd eyes to fee
Such order from confufion fprung,
Such gaudy tulips rais'd from *dung*. *Swift.*

To DUNG. *v. a.* [from the noun.] To manure with dung.

It was received of old, that *dunging* of grounds when the weft wind bloweth, and in the decreafe of the moon, doth greatly help. *Bacon's Nat. Hift.*

There, as his dream foretold, a cart he found,
That carried compoft forth to *dung* the ground.
Dryden.

DUʹNGEON. *n. f.* [from *donjon*, the tower

Definition of 'dung' from Johnson's *Dictionary* (1785).

'artificial sunshine' – for flower and fruit development. A balanced diet containing all of these nutrients makes plants good to look at and to eat, and helps them resist depredations.

The earliest surviving (idealised) building and landscape plan, dating from about AD 820, was probably the work of Abbot Haito of Reichnau, in present-day Switzerland, for St Gall monastery. It offers the perfect template for spiritual and physical self-sufficiency. In AD 840 Walahfrid Strabo, who became Bishop of Reichenau at the age of 30, wrote *Hortulus – the Little Garden*, which was transcribed in AD 875 at St Gall. It reads like the Bible, and includes the worthy advice: 'If you do not refuse to harden or dirty your hands . . . to spread whole baskets of dung on the sun-parched soil – then, you may rest assured, your soil will not fail you.' Dung was certainly to hand, for as pilgrims progressed to the great door of the monastery, behind a wall to their right were shelters and pens for sheep, goats, pigs, cows and horses, with similar accommodation for the servitors. Within the monastery walls stood a large stable and two further enclosures, one for mares and the other for bulls. By the wortyard or garden in the south-east corner were two circular runs with round fowl-houses for geese and chickens, with a central dwelling for their human caretakers.

The nuances of language can provide insights into the way a nation views its produce and products, and like the English the French might discuss dung in the general term *excrément*. More specifically, horse droppings are *crottin*, and *crotte* can apply to dung on the road or in the garden; cow pats are *bouse*, and my hero the dung beetle is a *bousier*. Wild animal dung and manure are *fumées* and *fumier* respectively, which are splendidly appropriate (odourmatopoeic?), while birds drop *de la fiente*.

Awash with nineteenth-century certainty, Shirley Hibberd wrote:

> Among other solid manures, night soil and guano may be noticed. The first is a very powerful fertiliser, and can still be had in many country districts, though our big towns are all busy in devising schemes to waste it. London, especially, might contribute to the soil around her

manure worth two millions a year, yet the Boards that manage these things are busying their wooden heads to throw it into the sea. Mr Schubbler thus estimates the relative value of night soil: 'If a given quantity of land sown without manure yields three times the seed employed, then the same quantity of land will produce five times the quantity sown when manured with old herbage, putrid grass or leaves, garden stuff, etc.; seven times with cow-dung, nine times with pigeons' dung, ten times with horse-dung, twelve times with human urine, twelve times with goats' dung, twelve times with sheep's dung, and fourteen times with human manure, or bullocks' blood; but if the land be of such quality as to yield without manure five times the quantity sown, then the horse-dung manure will yield fourteen, and human manure nineteen and two-thirds the sown quantity.'

Sadly, Mr Schubbler omitted to mention the figures that resulted from 'mix and match' excreta.

The focus of this book is the positive, amusing and constructive collection and use of dung. However, before analysing the good sources, it should be noted that insect dung mostly makes your heart sink. The bright red and lethal lily beetle can produce 200–300 grubs that will annihilate your lilies and fritillaries. In addition they have the temerity to chew the leaves and excrete

disgusting gunge over those that remain, disappearing from sight with a nifty backward roll as you approach to pick them off. (I now cup my hand under the leaf and stem before taking any other action, and then carry my prey to the execution block. I take no prisoners.)

When it comes to plums, the excessively unpleasant larvae of the plum sawfly (*Hoplocampa flava*) tunnel into the fruitlets while the pink and red caterpillars of the plum fruit moth (*Cydia funebrana*) bore into the ripening fruits. Satiated, they defecate in unmistakable spotty trails. The first luscious juicy bite is wholly ruined by a bitter aftertaste and visual displeasure.

Greenfly are a major garden pest and some say the same of the ant, with which it has an extraordinary coprophilic relationship. Greenfly have needle-like mouth parts that puncture plants to extract the sugary sap, and as they suck they excrete a sugary liquid. Ants move among the greenfly stroking their legs to squeeze out more sappy excreta, which they devour at source. Meanwhile, in the spring bees on their first warm day flight from the hive finally get the chance to uncross their legs, and lines of spring washing spotted with inconvenient and irritating deposits. Finally, we should note a recycling bug, the millipede, which recycles its tiny faecal pellets into building material for a nest for its eggs.

3

HUMAN MOTIONS

With rapturous ease men's cares shall flow away when seated at Convenience.

Josiah Feable (c.1855)

Prayers and Supplications

'Dust to dust' could equally be translated as 'dung to dung', in the sense that decomposition feeds the soil. For a nation on the move Moses gave sensible and sanitary advice: 'Thou shalt have a place without the camp to which thou mayst go for the necessities of nature, carrying a paddle at thy girdle. And, when thou sittest down, thou shalt dig round about and, with the earth that is dug up, thou shalt cover that which thou art eased of.' His advice is scrupulously ignored by SAS men and commandos on missions, who carry away with them all waste to ensure they leave no trail by which they might be traced. Astronauts settle on air-flushed lavatories that suck away the waste as it leaves the body; the liquids evaporate, but the solids are freeze-dried, sealed in packs and returned to Earth. But for less exalted folk, there remains the problem of effective disposal and, ideally, good use of our dung. In *Natural Theology* Kipling explores the idea of blaming someone else for all your ills, not least for the workings of your stomach. Taking the Primitive verses first:

> I ate my fill of a whale that died
> And stranded after a month at sea . . .

> There is a pain in my inside.
> Why have the Gods afflicted me?
> Ow! I am purged till I am a wraith!
> Wow! I am sick till I cannot see!
> What is the sense of Religion and Faith?
> Look how the Gods have afflicted me!

The cry of the pagan is followed by a medieval moan:

> My privy and well drain into each other
> After the custom of Christendie . . .
> Fevers and fluxes are wasting my mother.
> Why has the Lord afflicted me?
> The Saints are helpless for all I offer –
> So are the clergy I used to fee.
> Henceforward I keep my cash in my coffer,
> Because the Lord has afflicted me.

The Conclusion's final line runs 'Only Thyself hath afflicted thee!' The workings of our stomachs have exercised many minds with acres of advice. While blaming God and the devil for their ills, the hapless could also dwell on words attributed to John Harington, originator of the water-closet:

> A godly father, sitting on a draught
> To do as need and nature hath us taught,
> Mumbled (as was his manner) certain prayers,
> And unto him the devil straight repairs,
> And boldly to revile him he begins,
> Alleging that such prayers were deadly sin
> And that he shewed he was devoid of grace
> To speak to God from so unmeet a place.
> The reverent man, though at first dismayed,
> Yet strong in faith, to Satan thus he said:
> Thou damned spirit, wicked, false and lying,
> Despairing thine own good, and ours envying,

Each take his due, and me thou canst not hurt,
To God my prayer I meant, to thee the dirt.
Pure prayer ascends to Him that high doth sit,
Down falls the filth, for fiends of hell more fit.

In her book *Castaway* Lucy Irvine recalled a year spent on Tuin Island between Australia and New Guinea, and included an account of the status and use of lavatories on the nearby island of Badu. She wrote that, like God and the common cold, lavatories arrived in 1871. Holes were dug away from the main settlement and disguised with picturesque, palm-thatched houses locally known as 'pee-pee ouse'. The islanders, gregarious in their habits, rapidly resited the new structures to a more public location fronted by a generous area of raked sand. When the chief needed to perform, a conch would be sounded from a palm tree to invite the villagers to converge respectfully at the site. Irvine also reported that one headman took advantage of the situation by regularly taking an intolerably long time, so that he could hold forth to his rapt audience. They retaliated by returning to the old ways in the bush with a banana leaf.

In recent times the Australian government updated the houses with chipboard, corrugated iron, black rubber cans and doors. The cans are checked daily by the 'Numbawan s'it fella' for maggots and goanna or carpet pythons. When, as Irvine wrote, 'the yellow, heaving mass reaches within an inch of the top of a can', he puts on the lid and lifts the can into his tractor trailer. He has the constant companionship of a gang of joyriding ladies and at the end of the day they head for the sea. Up-current the ladies bathe and down-current Badu's Numbatwo floats off to Papua New Guinea!

When in City Pent

Market gardens flourished around the outer perimeters of the ancient Greek city states, and even Jerusalem had its 'dung port' without the city walls, beyond the gate of the valley. Columella advised Romans to 'bring as food for new-ploughed fallow-ground whatever stuff the privy vomits from its filthy sewers'. The main latrine at Housesteads Fort on Hadrian's Wall in Northumberland offered wooden seats for twenty and a fresh water channel into which they could dip sponge sticks in lieu of paper. The faecal trough and channel were flushed by rainwater and the effluent distributed on to nearby market gardens. From medieval times efficient recycling was undertaken by 'rakers' or 'gong-fermors', who were paid to collect waste and then sold it on. It could be a dangerous job, as in the case of Richard the Raker who died 'monstrously in his own excrement' in 1348.

This taunt to Lambeth gardeners was noted in 1607:

Foh, you nasty dogs that get your bread by the drippings of other people's fundaments; well you pray for the dunghill, for if that should fail, no turd, no gardener. Who was that, you rogues, that dung'd his own cap at stocks-market, and carried home the old gold to enrich his radish-bed?

Alms deeds and Pilgrim's salve were slang terms for excreta kindly donated by beggars to their fellow men, hence the medieval joke: 'Whether it is better to live by theft or by alms deeds?' Answer: 'The reward of theft is to be hanged; and if thou live by alms deeds, that is by beggars' turds.' (This was an adult version of the children's riddle 'Would you rather run a mile, jump a stile or eat a country pancake' – the country pancake being a cowpat.)

Accurate translation of historic documents is fraught with difficulties, but the Latin words *fossatum*, *fossata* and, occasionally, *fossatus* (all originally derived from a word meaning 'ditch') are used in medieval documents relating to land drainage. This technical name for any watercourse or artificial channel whose primary purpose was land drainage was, and is, rendered as 'sewer', as, for example, in the Norfolk Court of Sewers and the many historic 'Commissions of Sewers' found especially in Fenland and on the Romsey Marsh. Buyers of French country properties will know that their 'fosse septique' is their septic tank. Readers of Nancy Mitford's *The Pursuit of Love* will recollect the father's damning description of people, especially Non-Us, as sewers.

To us sewers are more than watercourses and their construction is essential to healthy, stench-free living. The Edenic picture of country living is the sweet scent of the hedgerows, careless rapture, paradise for John Milton's Eve, 'Veil'd in a cloud of fragrance, where she stood . . . among thick-woven arborets, and flowers Imborder'd on each bank'. She, of course, was watched enviously by the spirited sly snake, 'as one who long in populous city pent, Where houses thick and sewers annoy the air'.

The lost paradise was echoed exactly 150 years later by Keats in his sonnet addressed 'To one who has been long in city pent'. Over the centuries wealthy families were in the fortunate position of wintering in town and summering in the country and travelling to friends in between, thus avoiding 'Hyde Park Gardens, and the costly squares and streets adjacent, [where] the sewers abound with the foulest deposit, from which the most disgusting effluvium arises'.

The infamous nineteenth-century pollution of London was the result of millions of chimneys belching out smoke and inadequate drains haemorrhaging into its rivers. They weren't always so polluted. In the 1590s John Gerard the herbalist had gardens along the banks of the Fleet river where he grew more than a thousand varieties of plants. But by the 1720s Alexander Pope could write in the *Dunciad*: 'Where the Fleet-ditch with disemboguing streams, Rolls the large tribute of dead dogs to the Thames.' By 1840 the river was known simply as the Fleet Ditch, and when it was excavated for the building of St Pancras station its true awfulness was revealed:

> The Fleet Sewer affair involved the taking up of a main artery of metropolitan drainage, the diversion of a miniature Styx, whose black and foetid torrent had to be transferred from its bed of half-rotten bricks to an iron tunnel running in an entirely different direction, and that, too, without the spilling of 'one drop of Christian' sewage.

Eighteenth-century gentlemen had chamber-pots in the dining-room so they did not need to leave the room. At least the one in the right-hand corner of Hogarth's engraving has a lid. Sometimes there were several pots, and in private houses perhaps a screen to with-draw behind. *The Midnight Conversation*, William Hogarth (1733)

In 1842 Edwin Chadwick published his *Report on the Sanitary Condition of the Labouring Population of Great Britain*, which makes far from pleasant reading. A glimpse of London's seamier side is recorded in the words of Mr Howell, a civil engineer. (One wonders if he was the inspiration for this limerick:

> There once was a builder named Howell
> Who had a remarkable bowel.
> He built him a building
> Of brickwork and gilding
> Using – what do you think? – on his trowel.)

Howell's inspection of two properties was far from gilded:

> Upon visiting the latter, I found whole areas of the cellars of both houses were full of night soil to the depth of three feet, which had been permitted for years to accumulate from the overflow of the cesspools. . . . Upon passing through the passage of the first house I found the yard covered in a night soil from the overflowing of the privy to the depth of nearly 6 inches and bricks were placed to enable the inmates to get across dry shod.

There was nothing new about this. Pepys wrote in his diary for 20 October 1660: 'Going down to my cellar . . . I put my feet into a great heap of turds, by which I find that Mr Turner's house of office is full and comes into my cellar.'

In 1848 the control of London's drainage was vested in a Board of Commissioners, whose first task was to rid the city of cesspits, but the elderly sewers proved dire. Henry Mayhew's descriptions of the ordures of the sewers steam off the page:

> The deposit has been found to comprise all the ingredients from the breweries, the gas-works, and the several chemical and mineral manufactories; dead dogs, cats, kittens, and rats; offal from slaughter-houses, sometimes even including the entrails of the animals; street-pavement dirt of every variety; vegetable refuse; stable-dung; the refuse of pig-styes; night-soil; ashes; tin kettles and pans (panshreds); broken stoneware, as jars, pitchers, flower-pots etc.; bricks; pieces of wood; rotten mortar and rubbish of different kinds; and even rags.

Mayhew also identified the sewer-hunters, the poorest of the poor, who made their living by sifting through the above mix in the hopes of finding something to sell. One other deeply unpleasant occupation was collecting dogs' muck to sell to tanneries – was it worse for the tanners?

Also in 1848 11-year-old Thomas Crapper walked from Yorkshire to London and gained employment with a master plumber in Robert Street, Chelsea. He was to have a huge and lasting

Superstition has it that it is good luck to tread in dog muck without realising it until later, and that it is even luckier if you are barefooted. It is a matter of opinion.

influence on the condition of lavatories in London and through-out the British empire.

Soot and night-soil, adequately handled, were valuable com-modities, and according to Mayhew's social survey *London Labour and the London Poor* there were 800 sweeps operating in London in 1850. At night many of them exchanged their brushes for the even less glamorous job of carting away large buckets brimming with the contents of London's lavatories. The standard of town sanitation was far lower than that of the countryside, largely owing to the greater population, overcrowding in slum areas and the lack of an efficient network of drains.

These and other social deprivations were highlighted in the works of Charles Dickens – imagine the smell of Fagin's slum in *Oliver Twist* or the ordure cleared by Jo, the crossing sweeper, in *Bleak House*. Mayhew continues into Dickens territory:

A sewer from the Westminster Workhouse, which was of all shapes and sizes, was in so wretched a condition that the leveller could scarcely work for the thick scum that covered the glasses of the spirit-level in a few minutes after being wiped . . . a chamber is reached about 30 feet in length, from the roof of which hangings of putrid matter like stalactites descend three feet in length. At the end of this chamber, the sewer passes under the public privies, the ceilings of which can be seen from it. Beyond this it is not possible to go. . . .

On the 12th January we were very nearly losing a whole party by choke damp, the last man being dragged out on his back through two feet of black foetid deposits in a stage of insensibility.

The new jerry-built back-to-back houses lacked ventilation and drainage, with as many as twenty dwellings sharing one pump and one privy. The older city houses were desperately over-crowded: the ninety-five dwellings in the old London rookery of St Giles contained some 2,850 people. Even the better sort of

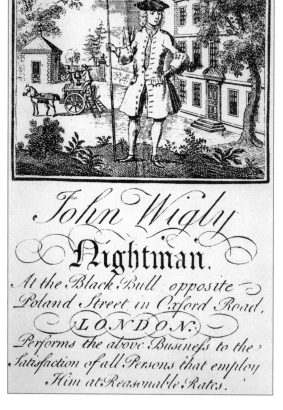

John Wigly's tradecard portraying a rather rosy view of his job as an eighteenth-century nightman. It cost about a shilling to have your cesspit emptied at a time when the average weekly wage was 3s. After rent, food and other expenses it was all too easy to let the weeks slip by. (© Mary Evans Picture Library)

urban houses still relied on a cesspit either in the cellar or under the ground floor but these, as mentioned above, were not infrequently allowed to overflow. In well-ordered and solvent homes the contents were regularly carried away in buckets by 'Night Men', such as the sweeps mentioned above. Henry Hastings, 'Nightman & Poleman For the City and Suburbs', was one such. He was based in Southwark and his business card assured his potential customers that he 'decently performs what He undertakes being always at the work himself. Empties Vaults & Cesspools, unstops Tunnels & Cleans Drains at the very Lowest Prices. Any Gentleman Sending a line shall be waited on at the Shortest Notice. NB I have the new invented Machine Carts for the Quick dispatch of Business.' He also offered to clean and dig wells.

Cholera

In Sunderland in 1831 a deadly epidemic broke out. It was characterised by violent vomiting and rice-coloured evacuations which drained the body of nutrients and fluids, leading to dehydration, kidney failure and often death within hours. Malignant cholera had arrived from India. Although the increased use of water closets had improved domestic sanitation, there was no equivalent onward removal system and, of course, cholera was transmitted through the faeces of the sufferers. As Thomas Cubitt sarcastically reported in 1840: 'Fifty years ago nearly all London had every house cleansed into a large cesspool. . . . Now sewers have been very much improved, scarcely any person thinks of making a cesspool, but it is carried off at once into the river. The Thames is now made a great cesspool instead of each person having one of his own.'

Cholera reached London later in 1831, and 6,636 people died. A further outbreak between 1848 and 1849 killed 14,137 people. Referring to London in 1849 *The Spectator* reported: 'We are paying the [water] companies collectively £340,000 per annum for a more or less concentrated solution of native guano.' That year Dr John Snow, a pioneer anaesthetist working in Soho, published

On the Mode of Communication of Cholera, in which he put forward the theory that it was water-borne. He proposed that the flushing of sewage into rivers should be stopped, and that there should be two supplies of water, one metered and clean for drinking and one for flushing. Snow had his eye on a particular well in Broad Street near Golden Square in Soho. It was perilously close to a sewer, and he was convinced that the water had been contaminated by seeping sewage. He then identified cholera-infected water from a pump in Broadwick Street off Carnaby Street. Today the site is graced by a granite memorial to him and you can toast his health at the nearby John Snow pub. Between 1853 and 1854 a further 10,738 people died, but Snow's theory was rejected by the Committee for Scientific Enquiry. In 1866 a further 5,596 people died in the East End in another outbreak. Cholera was also a recurring problem in the new industrial towns, where, for example, between 1861 and 1881 the population of Salford rose by 72 per cent and that of Leicester by 80 per cent, while by 1865 the population of Widnes had reached 10,000 – with no public sewer. A poster appeared in Dudley:

> CHOLERA. The Dudley Board of Health hereby give notice, that in consequence of the Church-yards at Dudley Being so full, no one who has died of the CHOLERA will be permitted to be buried after SUNDAY next (Tomorrow) in either of the Burial Grounds of *St Thomas's*, or *St Edmund's*, in this Town. All Persons who die from CHOLERA must for the future be buried in the Church-yard at Netherton.
>
> BOARD OF HEALTH, DUDLEY

It was not until 1883 that the German bacteriologist Robert Koch identified the *vibrio cholerae*, commonly known as comma bacillus in India. He had already identified the organisms that cause anthrax and tuberculosis, and in 1905 he was awarded the Nobel Prize for Medicine. One of our family legends concerns my maternal great-grandparents who lived in Hamburg, where my great-grandmother drank a whole bottle of whisky to protect her from a devastating cholera outbreak. While researching this book

The oak wreaths suggest that the artist is depicting the anniversary of Charles II's restoration on 29 May. A chamber-pot is being emptied from the upper window, and the nightman is emptying someone's barrel into his larger receptacle. Smoking may be regarded today as unhealthy, but it masked the stench – and the practice was still popular in privies in the twentieth century. *The Four Times of the Day – Night*, William Hogarth (1738)

(Sanitary Inspector, Malling Union stamp)

Aylesford, Maidstone
Sept. 8th 1874

Mr Collins
Sir,

Having visited Back Street, West Malling yesterday with Dr Baylis I have to call your attention to the state of the privy on your property and to ask you to have it emptied. The Rabbits and Pigs are in much too confined quarters for the health of the Inhabitants and must be done away with altogether.

Yours Obdtly.
S. Wagon

P.S. In a few days I will send you a new plan of privy, approved of by the Sanitary Authority

(Sanitary Inspector, Malling Union stamp)

Aylesford, Maidstone
29th Oct. 1874

Mr Collins
Dear Sir,

I have to call your attention to the state of the privies on your property in Back Street, West Malling in the occupation of Selby & others and as they are in a dilapidated state I must ask you to erect others. I believe I sent you a short time since the plan of a privy approved by the Medical Officer.

I have been very busy lately and have not had an opportunity of inspecting your other property in Back St., but when I do I hope to see the nuisances I called your attention

The letters (*opposite*) enclosing the plan for an earth closet privy (*right and below*) are from the Sanitary Inspector, Malling Union, at Aylesford, Maidstone, in Kent. They were sent to Henry Collings who was a draper in West Malling (his shop is now part of the County Library). He married his housekeeper in his 60th year and they had four children. The family lived with the rabbits and pigs at Back Street, West Malling. The privy was installed, but is long gone; the house still stands. (*Anne Meads*)

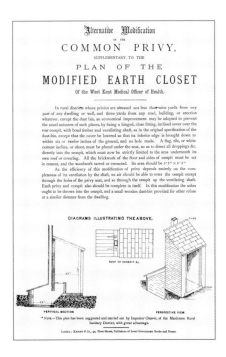

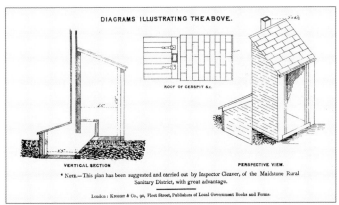

I learnt that in Hamburg in 1892 no fewer than 8,605 people died during this outbreak in a city that was one-seventh the size of London. Cholera is of course water-borne and the appalling seepage of sewage into drinking water supplies in urban areas was the culprit. Something had to be done.

The Great Stink

The denizens of the magnificent new Palace of Westminster designed by Charles Barry and Auguste Pugin in 1840 dared not open the windows along the riverside because of the stench, while walking Parliament's terraces was impossible. The *Quarterly Review* published a damning attack:

> Like another Troy, this citadel of filth has stood a ten years' siege: and its sturdy garrison, led by their chieftains in Common Council – the Hectors and Memnons of intramural muck – so far from thinking of surrender, are engaged at this moment in fortifying their defences. The Defenders of Filth, corporate and parochial, have ruled London long enough.

In the exceptionally hot and dry summer of 1858 the Thames and its foetid city tributaries shrank, and the stench grew ever worse, backwashed twice daily by the tides. The London Stink of 1858 was so bad that MPs even discussed transferring Parliament elsewhere. On 2 August the Metropolis Local Management Amendment Act was passed, giving the Metropolitan Board of Works power to borrow £300,000 (guaranteed by the Treasury) to carry out main drainage work. This sum would be repaid from the proceeds of a 3d rate to be levied over forty years. In 1863 they raised a further £1,200,000. *The Times* advocated a directly elected body which 'would have strength enough to double the work of Hercules and to cleanse not only the filthy stables but the river which runs through them'. At which point enter our hero, Joseph William Bazalgette.

Born in Enfield, Middlesex, in 1819, Bazalgette was one of the most notable pioneers of public health engineering. In the 1860s, as chief engineer to the Board of Works, he proposed a network of sewers running parallel with the river, which would intercept and carry away both waste and surface water. In 1865 some 83 miles of large intercepting sewers were opened; draining over 100 square miles of buildings, they carried some 420 million gallons a day. The outfalls were well away from London, at Crossness near Plumstead on the south side of the river and at Barking on the north side. Lambeth and Pimlico were actually below the high-tide level so their sewage had to be lifted by gravity. The system to the north was complex, with three main intercepting sewers known as High, Middle and Low, the latter two both having branches. All were built of Staffordshire Blue bricks, which were high baked and strong and could resist the scouring motion. The High Sewer ran 9 miles to Hampstead Heath and Old Ford, Stratford; using the River Lea, it was constructed 20–26ft underground with a fall of 4ft per mile. The Middle Sewer was up to 36ft deep; running from Kensal Green to the junction with the High Sewer at Old Ford, with a branch to Piccadilly, it ran parallel to the Gray's Inn Road for a total of 12 miles. The Low Sewer included not only sewers but also subways, the Metropolitan Underground line, gas pipes and other services, all contained under the magnificent Victoria Embankment. The 12-mile long system started at Pimlico and followed the river to Vauxhall Bridge, then on to Westminster Bridge and Blackfriars, before turning north under Queen Victoria Street, Tower Hill, Cable Street and Bow. A tunnel took it under the River Lea. Branches also went out beyond the docks and the Isle of Dogs. Above ground the market gardeners in the Lea Valley daily delivered wagons of fresh produce, returning home with money to pay their bills and darker gold to feed their soil.

Subscribers to the *City Press* in 1864 were told: 'Not to know the particulars of the latest movements on the sewage question is to be quite unfit for the drawing-room where scientific and social subjects are freely mingled in the elements of elegant conversation.' But twenty years later in 1885 *The Times* thundered: 'Anybody who has frequented the Thames would, though he has been years away and returned blind, recognise its stream by the dull brooding atmosphere of odours the Metropolitan Board of Works brews from its London sewage.' Just think what it might have been like!

Bazalgette also built the Albert Embankment and the Victoria Embankment, and as a consequence of his new sewage system the death rate in London had started to decline by the 1870s.

One of Thames Water's sludge boats is called SS *Bazalgette*. In 1995 Thames Water 'exported' 4.3 megawatts of electricity to the National Grid from their CoGaS (Combined Gas and Steam) plant at Barking, generating the power by igniting the methane gas in sewage. Following the ban of marine disposal of waste in 1998, advanced incineration plants were built at Barking and Crossness. They compress the sludge recovered from settlement tanks at treatment works and incinerate it through a sand bed at 850°C. The heat generated is recovered and used to drive a steam turbine. This provides electricity to run the treatment works and the substantial surplus of power is 'exported' to the National Grid. The remaining liquid is treated by an aerobic process that promotes bacterial activity to remove impurities and then the treated liquid is released into the Thames. A small amount of the incinerated ash is marketed as breeze blocks.

Temples of Convenience

In 1844 Queen Victoria, Prince Albert, their children and retainers suffered a series of unpleasant sore throats and other ailments at Windsor Castle. Albert investigated with Teutonic efficiency and found no fewer than fifty-three overflowing cesspits fed by the castle's outmoded Hanoverian commodes. The very latest in water-closets and drains were installed immediately. At about the same time, in one of the reports leading up to the 1848 Public Health Act, the streets of Windsor were described as follows: 'From the gas-works at the end of George Street a double line of open, deep, black and stagnant ditches extends to Clewer-lane. From these ditches an intolerable stench is perpetually rising, and produces fever of a severe character.' The seamy side of Cambridge has already been highlighted and the River Cam features in Gwen Raverat's book *Period Piece* about her childhood there:

> I can remember the smell very well, for all the sewage went into the
> river, till the town was at last properly drained, when I was about ten

years old. There is a tale of Queen Victoria being shown over Trinity by the Master, Dr Whewell, and saying, as she looked down over the bridge: 'What are all those pieces of paper floating down the river?' To which, with great presence of mind, he replied: 'Those, ma'am, are notices that bathing is forbidden.'

Albert's enthusiasm for modern technology was channelled into the Great Exhibition of 1851, which provided a showcase for 14,000 exhibitors. It opened on 1 May in Hyde Park, London, and was housed in what was described by Ruskin as 'a greenhouse larger than ever greenhouse was built before'. Punch sarcastically christened it the Crystal Palace.

Knighthoods were duly bestowed on the contractor Charles Fox, the designer Joseph Paxton, and the builder Thomas Cubitt, but the unsung hero was George Jennings, a man who was not afraid to mention the unmentionable. Jennings was responsible for installing the public lavatories for the Exhibition, attracting payment from 827,280 users of the 'waiting-rooms'. And 'in addition, a larger proportion of gentlemen used the urinals, of which no account was kept. No apology is needed for publishing these facts which demonstrate the sufferings which must be endured by all, but especially by the females on account of the want of them.' On 11 October, after 6,039,195 visitors had passed through the turnstiles, the Exhibition closed to the public.

After some debate the Crystal Palace was dismantled and re-erected at Sydenham, but the public conveniences were not included, on the grounds of cost and that 'persons would not come to Sydenham to wash their hands'. Jennings campaigned hard to have the lavatories installed and won, and his installations duly produced a revenue of £1,000 a year. In 1858 Jennings undertook his third cleansing crusade against 'those Plague Spots that are offensive to the eye, and a reproach to the Metropolis', demanding the provision of 'conveniences suited to this advanced stage of civilisation'. The conveniences, known as 'Halting Stations', were to be constructed underground and would be manned by respectable attendants, and Jennings offered to bear all the costs of construction in return for being allowed to charge a small fee. His proposal highlights the delicacy of Victorian values:

> I know the subject is a peculiar one, and very difficult to handle, but no false delicacy ought to prevent immediate attention being given to matters affecting the health and comfort of the thousands who daily throng the thoroughfares of your City . . . the Civilisation of a People can be measured by their Domestic and Sanitary appliances and although my proposition may be startling I am convinced the day will come when Halting Stations replete with every convenience will be constructed in all localities where numbers assemble. Fancy one of these complete, having a respectable attendant, who on pain of dismissal should be obliged to give each seat a rub over with a damp leather after use, the same attendant to hand a clean towel, comb and brush to those who may require to use them.

Jennings would have been delighted to know that in the 1990s the attendant in the Cambridge Lion Yard public conveniences was a great book collector and his room was lined with signed first editions. Conveniently the ambient temperature was perfect for the books and the collection was securely locked up at night.

But Jennings' offer was spurned: 'My offer (I blush to record it) was declined by Gentlemen (influenced by English delicacy of feeling) who preferred that the Daughters and Wives of English-men should encounter at every corner, sights so disgusting to every sense, and the general Public suffers pain and often perm-anent injury rather than permit the construction of that shelter and privacy now common in every City in the World.' In 1855 Jennings' plans were at last realised with the first underground public convenience in the world. Josiah Feable commemorated the event with a poem that was inscribed on a plaque and read by him to the queen at Windsor:

> I' front the Royal Exchange, and Underground,
> Down gleaming walls of Porc'lain flows the sluice
> That out of sight decants the kidney Juice,

> Thus pleasuring those Gents for miles around,
> Who, crying for relief, once piped the Sound
> Of Wind in alleyways. All hail this news!
> And let the joyous shuffling queues
> For gentlemanly Jennings' most well-found
> Construction, wherein a Penny opens the gate
> To Heav'n's mercy; and sanitary Wares
> Receive the Gush with seemly cool obedience,
> Enthroning Queen Hygeia in blessed state
> on Crapper's rocket: with rapturous ease men's cares
> Shall flow away when seated at Convenience!

One wonders if Victoria was entertained or appalled. However, by the 1870s the authorities were beginning to implement Jennings's ideas with enthusiasm – and now, as we embark on the third millennium, they are equally busy dismantling them!

Jennings went on to win the Gold Medal Award at the 1884 Health Exhibition with his 'Pedestal Vase'. Its 2-gallon flushing

A ratcatcher working in London's sewers in about 1870. These men were shunned and feared for their association with filth and contagion. At about the same time Paris was under siege during the Franco-Prussian War and the starving citizens were forced to eat rats to avoid starvation. (© Mary Evans Picture Library)

power was tested using ten apples averaging 1¼in in diameter, a flat sponge about 4½in across, some plumber's 'smudge' coated over the pan and four pieces of paper adhering closely to the soil surface (what does this say about Victorian bowel movements?). Mr Shanks, also competing, simply flushed down an attendant apprentice's cap.

Of course, no discussion of lavatories would be complete without mention of Thomas Crapper (1837–1910). Contrary to popular opinion, however, his name did not give us the term 'crap', which actually derives from the Old French *crappe* meaning siftings. (It could also be used to refer to offscourings or dregs of ale, fat residues, and chaff or husk of grain.) Its use was first recorded in 1493, but by the end of the medieval period its definition had widened to include rubbish and ordure, and by 1846 it meant to defecate. After thirteen years working in London, Crapper set up the Marlboro' Works of Thomas Crapper & Co. in Marlborough Road, Chelsea. His company plumbed clients' outflow drainage into Bazalgette's new sewer system. The water-closets available at the time used copious (and sometimes continuous) amounts of precious water, but the cistern on Crapper's new Valveless Water Waste Preventer set up a siphonic action of 'considerable velocity'. This not only saved water but was almost soundless. His company thrived. Thomas Crapper & Co. was granted no less than four royal warrants in the following fifty years by Edward VII as Prince of Wales and by King George V as Prince of Wales and king. Veritable thrones, Crapper's 'Rockets' were named after the streets in the royal borough in which he worked, hence: Marlboro, Onslow, Walton, Lennox, Ovington, Manresa, Cadogan, Culford and Sloane.

Waste Not, Want Not

In 1856 the Metropolitan Board of Works invited entrepreneurs to propose schemes to use sewage. This resulted in the short-lived 'Native Guano Company' which operated from 1871 to 1873. Following London's example, Paris had created an embankment along the River Seine to ease bodily movements over and underground. The *Leisure Hour* of 1885 carried an article on 'The Harvest of the River Seine', with the subtitle 'A notable instance of obtaining wealth from waste'. It was illustrated with a chiffonnier, not a piece of furniture but a sort of rag-and-bone man, whose occupation was very similar to that of Mayhew's sewer-hunters except that he worked along the banks of the Seine rather than in the bowels of the sewers. The journalist's article was based on M. Paulian's book about the chiffonnier's basket, and both quote Victor Hugo, who was one of the first to draw attention to the untapped wealth in *Les Misérables*:

> Paris throws into the water every year twenty-five millions of francs! This is no metaphorical statement, but simple truth. How, and in what fashion? By night and by day. With what purpose? With no purpose. With what thought? With no thought. To do what? To do nothing. By what agency? By the sewerage of the city. . . .

In churchyards, feeding cattle, playing games, depositing dung, emptying chamber-pots and answering the call of nature were roundly and soundly condemned, resulting in injunctions against the perpetrators. Was this a ruined church or an eyecatcher?

He describes the Chinese recycling of sewerage as blessing them with a land that looks as young as it did at the time of Abraham or Noah. In Edenic prose that seems to echo the re-establishment of the church in France, he continues:

> European nations send fleets to the New World to bring over costly guano, while neglecting greater wealth at home. It is not pleasant to think of the sewerage of a great city; but to the eye of science, when opened, this uncleanness means green grain and flowery meadows; it means thyme and marjoram and all fragrant herbs; it means sweet-smelling hay and golden harvests; it means bread on your table and meat in your larder; it means warm blood in your veins; it means health, and joy, and life! Such is the result of that marvellous creation, which is transformation on earth and transfiguration in heaven. Put this waste into your crucible, and abundance will come out. The fertilising of the fields becomes the nourishment of men. It is not from Paris only, but from all the great centres of population, and by every river of France, that this wealth is carried to the sea, enough to pay a quarter of the expense of the national budget! Thus we show our knowledge and skill, with the twofold result of impoverishing the land and polluting the water, encouraging hunger in our fields and disease in our rivers.

The sewerage described included a great deal more than dung disgorging onto the banks of the Seine. During 1883 the following corpses were also washed up: 4,293 dogs, 5 calves, 20 sheep, 7 goats, 7 pigs, 80 poultry, 68 cats, 955 rabbits, 13 fish, 1 monkey and 1 serpent, but no account was kept of the carcasses of rats or 'small deer'. How did it all get there? The *Leisure Hour* enlightens:

> The sewerage of Paris, that enormous subterranean system, the result of ten centuries of labour, which has cost hundreds of millions of francs, and many a workman's life, is composed of more than eight hundred kilometres of galleries, the waters of which converge to one huge sewer, the Cloaca maxima of the capital, which joins the Seine near the bridge of Asnières. All the refuse of the city, all the dirty

water, all the rags and refuse which the chiffonnier has not seized, all the unclean waste of the houses and shops and streets, pass from the sinks and gutters to the sewers, and gradually these form a great river, which pours itself into the Seine.

The uses to which the 'debris' was put ranged from agricultural and horticultural fertiliser to the making of candles and coarse soap, and even raising maggots for fishing bait.

Have You Been?

Training young children to have regular habits occupies many a written page and results in much parental anxiety, sometimes to the point of obsession. In her excellent *Yesterday's Children* Sally Kevill-Davies describes the methods and the equipment used to instil regular habits in the young (the latter are now highly sought-after antiques!). The subtitle above is a quote from Andrew Combe, who wrote the confidence-inspiring *Treatise on the Physiological and Moral Management of Infancy* in 1840, addressing mothers in firm tones: 'They seem to regard the body as a machine acting upon no fixed principles, and requiring now and then to be

This little girl is in danger, and not only of being kicked. Horses defecate without a second thought, and are able to continue any activity unabated.

driven by some foreign impulse in the shape of medicine. Under this impression they are on the watch to see what they can do to keep it moving, and are altogether distrustful of the Creator's arrangement.' Poor mothers, ever the under-achievers! Combe's near-contemporary Mrs Balfour concurred: 'A dirty child is the Mother's Disgrace.' A friend of mine was so thrilled every time her small son performed in his potty that he began to lisp that he needed to do a 'splendid'. But tolerance, moderation and sense were the bywords for John Locke, famed for his empiricist philosophy expounded in an *Essay concerning Human Understanding*. In this context in 1693 he wrote in 'Some Thoughts Concerning Education' that bowel regularity could be achieved simply by telling children to 'go to stool' at the same time each day. Fear of diarrhoea and its worst consequences denied many children fresh fruit and, as Sally Kevill-Davies summarises: 'By the nineteenth century this diet had successfully ensured that the nurseries of England were crammed with children blocked solid with constipation, which was treated with dreaded home-made suppositories made from soap sticks, or enemas of soap and water, helped along by loosening draughts of castor oil washed down with peppermint water.' Calomel, another favourite, was a compound of the cumulative poison mercury.

Stool watching was a task of imperial importance from China to France, as depicted in one of the early scenes in the film *The Last Emperor*. Henry Ashby urged Victorian mothers to be equally vigilant for 'the stools of the infant should always be carefully watched, as important information . . . may be gathered from careful and continuous examination'. *Advice to a Mother on the Management of her Children and on the Treatment on the Moment of some of their more pressing illnesses and accidents* by Pye Henry Chavasse appeared in its tenth edition in 1870, by which time it had been translated into French, and published in London, New York and Paris, as well as in Australia and in India. There was even a Tamil edition. Chavasse praised and quoted Mrs Balfour on the iniquity of a 'dirty child'. The book takes a question and answer form, thus number 87:

Q. Have you any hints to offer respecting the bowels and the bladder of an infant during his first three months of existence?

A. Mother ought daily to satisfy herself as to the state of the bladder and bowels of her child. She herself should inspect the motions, and see that they are of a proper colour (bright yellow, inclining to orange), and consistence (that of thick gruel), that they are neither slimy, nor curdled, nor green; if they should be either the one or the other, it is a proof that she herself has, in all probability, been imprudent in her diet, and that it will be necessary for the future that she be more careful both in what she eats and in what she drinks.

For the record the colour of the stool is related to how long it has been in the intestine. A rapid transit time produces a green stool, a longer time makes it yellow, then brown, then black. If the stool contains blood, it is black, tarry and very foul-smelling. A friendly paediatrician told me that he was often approached by parents who were convinced their children had an infection because their stool was green. Dennis Burkitt, well known in medical circles for identifying Burkitt's Lymphoma, worked for years in Uganda. On his return in the late 1970s he lectured and published papers on Ugandan faeces versus European examples. He linked many European bowel and digestive complaints to the western reliance on processed foods and compared our diet to the fibre-rich foods eaten in Africa. Medical and consumer magazines carried coloured annotated illustrations with accompanying measurements to endorse his findings. Today several European countries have lavatories that afford adults the option of close inspection before flushing away the evidence.

Edward Mansfield Brockbank's 1912 advice would be viewed as child molestation today: 'tickling the anus, or introducing just inside the rectum a small cone of oiled paper, or a piece of soap, as a suggestion of the purpose for which the infant is placed on the chamber'. I was advised in 1980 that placing a small chamber-pot under my son every time I picked him up from birth would encourage 'solid' training by 3 weeks! However, I was a follower of Penelope Leach's *Baby & Child*: 'Don't try to tamper with the natural bowel pattern. Laxatives to make it "easier" or soap sticks to induce a motion at a convenient moment are totally wrong. It is his body.' But the written word is so much easier than the reality, and I would often chuckle at: 'Faeces in the pot deserve a quiet word about how grown up he is getting. Faeces in his nappy or on the floor need an equally quiet word about the possibility that he might choose to put them in the pot tomorrow.' A veritable Joyce Grenfell and George moment! The Birmingham Museums & Art Gallery has a delightful Scottish rocking commode chair for a child, complete with its original wooden chamber-pot. Gentle rocking was presumably thought to be conducive to bowel movement.

Busy Beetle

We return to the words of Henri Fabre, scientist and close observer of dung beetles, who wrote despairingly of the habits of the Provençal peasant by comparison to the ecological habits of geotrupes, a type of dung beetle. In the chapter entitled 'The Geotrupes' he recorded no fewer than four types, two of which he described as: 'Black as ink above, both of them magnificently garbed below. One is quite surprised to find such a jewel-case among the professional scavengers. Geotrupes Stercorarius is of a splendid amethyst violet on his lower surface, while Geotrupes Hypocrita is lavish with the ruddy gleams of copper pyrites.' Earlier he had bemoaned the unhygienic habits of the Provençal peasant, but to the rescue rode the Geotrupe, 'that faithful observer of the Mosaic edict. . . . It is his to remove from sight, it is his to bury the germ-crammed matter. Supplied with implements for digging far superior to the paddle . . . he hastens and, as soon as man is gone, digs a pit wherein the infection is swallowed up and rendered harmless.' Fascinated by their Herculean endeavours, Fabre collected Geotrupes and put them to work on mule and other droppings. Satisfied by their performance, he concluded that the Geotrupes are passionate buriers; they take underground a

deal more than is necessary for their consumption. As this work is performed, in varying degrees, by legions of collaborators, large and small, it is evident that the purification of the soil must benefit by it to an ample extent and that the public's health is to be congratulated on having this army of auxiliaries in its service. . . . What the Geotrupe buries and abandons the next day is not lost: far from it. Nothing is lost in the world's balance-sheet; the stock-taking total is constant. The little lump of dung buried by the insect will make the nearest tuft of grass grow a luxuriant green. A sheep passes and crops the bunch of grass: all the better for the leg of mutton which man is waiting for. The Dung-beetle's industry has procured us a savoury mouthful.

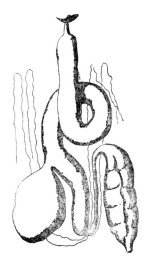

Digestive apparatus of the Sacred Beetle.

A Very Good Ornament to his Dwelling

Much of the soil that lies around our fifteenth-century cottage is dark and rich, in marked contrast to the indigenous heavy clay. Our antecedents had no indoor facilities and right up until the 1970s the bucket was emptied weekly into ready prepared trenches. During the first six months of our tenancy we did the same. On the rare occasions when our septic tank needs emptying, I am tempted to put all our healthy, familiar waste on to the garden but I do have to consider my neighbours and family. In December 2004 I was delighted to read Ursula Buchan's *Spectator* column eulogising the annual gift the former occupants of her now redundant two-seater brick privy had contributed to her soil and its continuing gardening triumphs.

Apophthegm is a splendid word for a pithy maxim, and I shall conclude this chapter with one by Francis Bacon: 'The Empirical philosophers are like to pismires; they only lay up and use their store. The Rationalists are like to spiders; they spin all out of their own bowels. But give me a philosopher who, like the bee, hath a middle facility gathering from abroad, but digesting that which is gathered by his own virtue.' Or even twentieth-century straight talking attributed to Ethel Merman, 'Life is like shit, you get back what you put in.'

4

PENNED FOR PROFIT

The men with the muck-rakes are often indispensable to the well-being of society; but only if they know when to stop raking the muck.

Theodore Roosevelt (1908)

Utile et Dulci

Pliny recommended sieving cattle dung so that it had 'a pleasant smell, and looketh lovely withal'. There is an element of truth in this because cows drink a lot of water and produce about ten soft cowpats a day, each of fine consistency. In many English tenures the flocks and herds of the tenants had to be folded on the lord's land at night – in what could be termed an early form of stealth tax. Medieval land agents reading Walter de Henley's *Husbandrie* were instructed on how to preserve dung by sealing it with litter and marl, a combination later referred to as manure. In his 1909 *Fertilizers and Manures* A.D. Hall quoted a French rhyme:

> Point de fourrage, point de betail,
> Point de betail, point de fumier,
> Point de fumier, point de fourrage.
> ('Without hay, no cattle,
> Without cattle, no manure,
> Without manure, no hay.')

Daniel Defoe travelled around early eighteenth-century England praising examples of *utile et dulci* as gardens and landscapes were being created to express English liberty (and provide profits), in contrast to the geometric rigidity of French landscapes. In 1728 Batty Langley provided an elaborate scheme for James Johnston in Twickenham. Instead of the 'regular, stiff, and stuft-up Manner' of French gardens he designed a 'rural garden' incorporating industrious agricultural or georgic elements. The same year Langley published his ideas in *New Principles of Gardening*:

> If we enter the Wilderness . . . we are led through their pleasant Meanders, with the agreeable Entertainments of Flower Gardens, Fruit Gardens, Orangerys, Groves, of Forest Trees, and Ever-Greens, Open-plains, Kitchen Gardens, Physick Gardens, Paddocks of Sheep, Deer, Cows, etc. Hop Grounds, Nurseries of Fruit and Forest Trees, Ever-Greens, &tc. Vineyards, Inclosures of Corn, Grass, Clover, etc. Cones of Fruit Trees, Forest Trees, Ever-Greens, Flowering Shrubs, Basins, Fountains, Canals, Cascades, Grottos, Warrens of Hares and Rabbets, Aviaries, Manazaries, Bowling-Greens; and those rural Objects, Hay-Stacks and Wood Piles, as in a Farmer's Yard in the Country. Which several Parts are disposed of in such a Manner, and Distance, as not to see, or know the next approaching, when we have seen the first, so that we are continually entertain'd with new unexpected Objects at every Step we take; for the Entrances into those Parts being made intricate, we can never know when we have seen the whole. Which (if I mistake not) is the true End and Design of laying out Gardens of Pleasure.

Langley penned for profit in every sense.

The picturesque Hameau de la Reine in the grounds of Versailles represents Marie-Antoinette's lasting legacy. She was only 15 in 1770 when she was brought to France to marry the future Louis XVI, and she rapidly grew to loathe court life, seeking instead to create a bucolic idyll on her model farm. She was inspired by the 'English village' designed by J.-F. Leroy for de Bourbon Condé at Chantilly. There were seven peasant cottages and a barn, complete with rustic exteriors and stunning interiors, around a village green, and guests were served Crème Chantilly from the dairy. In 1783 Mique designed Le Hameau de la Reine, with a dozen rustic thatched houses around a lake. Unlike their forerunners, they all had a farming purpose.

Both before and after the French Revolution the *jardin anglais* was all the rage in France, to the extent that in 1786 at Le Raincy the Duke of Orleans (Philippe Egalite) desired beauty and utility as an enlightened 'English' landowner surrounded by a prosperous and contented peasantry. France's 'Capability Brown' was a Scot, Thomas Blaikie, whose English landscaping contract included the usual excavations, digging up and logging trees and creating 1,200m of *allées* through woodland lined with sand and pebbles. Swiss cows, an English bull and their products were catered for in *la vacherie*, where ornamental cowhouses resembled Swiss chalets. Every tenant had a furnished dwelling with a well-manured garden, all overseen by another Scot, Alexander Howatson, as head gardener.

Marie-Josèphe-Rose Tascher de la Pagerie, known as Rose to her family, was just eight years younger than Marie-Antoinette. In 1779 she married General Alexandre Vicomte de Beauharnais, who died on the guillotine. On 9 March 1796 this Rose by another name, Josephine, married Napoleon Bonaparte. She was adorned with violets for their wedding day, and in romantic spirit Napoleon always presented her with violets on their anniversary. At Malmaison the Empress Josephine wanted an English garden and her own Petit Trianon, with hothouses for plants to remind her of her native Martinique. She too had a *vacherie* along the banks of the lake and appointed Howatson as head gardener. Sadly, in 1809 Napoleon repudiated her and the *vacherie* (and gardens) of Malmaison disappeared.

Long Straw

The value of an animal's excreta is dictated by age and diet. If penned on litter, the dung of sheep and horses is drier and richer than that of cows or pigs. Litter offered comfort, warmth and absorption, and in turn added organic matter and nitrogen to the manure. Throughout history leaves, bracken, fern, hopbine and peat moss have all been used as litter, the latter being especially prized for its capacity to absorb ten times more water than straw and remaining sweet for longer. However, straw was (and largely still is) the first choice for penned and stabled animals. Due to the prolonged growing season, wheat, oat and barley straw from the north of England and Scotland are richer in nitrogen, potash and phosphorus. Wheat straw, which can absorb two or three times its weight in water: was highly esteemed, with the added bonuses of being cleaner and wearing better underfoot. Oat straw runs a close second but barley straw tends to be brittle and dry.

The Revd Arthur Young was a keen travelling observer and chronicler, who in 1769 published *Six Weeks Tour Through the Southern Counties* which included a visit to Bury St Edmunds in Suffolk:

> Before I leave the neighbourhood of Bury I must observe, that I never met with any place around which the farmers had such a spirit of purchasing manures; very ordinary sorts sell at Bury at 2*s* 6*d* and 3*s* a waggon load of 80 bushels; I saw all round the town in different places heaps of purchased manures. . . . The importance of manuring, I found in general better understood than I expected. . . . About Bury . . . they purchase the manure arising in that town at a vast expense; and with such eagerness, that were the town half as big as London, they would buy them all. Between Sudbury and Braintree in Essex, they are very careful in forming composts of chalk, dung and turf.

Today a good load of manure costs about £40.

In 1996 the Revd S.A. Snelling published his memoirs. From 1920 to 1924 he worked as a teenager on a Suffolk farm, and he described the value of all straw (except oat) that was used for litter in cattle, horse and pig yards. During the winter the animals trod it into their manure to form muck, and when they were put out to grass in the spring the yards were cleared and the muck stacked

A Victorian children's illustration of biblical animals all of which have contributed to this book. The nutritious fig with its laxative syrup and a bunch of get-well-soon grapes may well have featured in the nursery. Less familiar is that the rind of the pomegranate can be used against diarrhoea and chronic dysentery, while the blessed thistle is valuable for debilitating conditions of the stomach. In *Rerum rusticarum* (36 BC) Varro assures his readers that 'no serpent breeds in the dung-hill if a piece of oakwood be driven into the middle of it'.

Left: The dovecote at Fanshawe Hall in Derbyshire is part of the original Tudor complex. Note the raised door to prevent rats entering. Today this decorative part of the gardens is filled with a stock of guano. *Right:* Varro would not have approved of the red dovecotes in the new Alnwick Garden, but the white doves provide an attractive contrast. *(Author's Collection)*

Rendall's Dovecote on the mainland Orkney Islands is of traditional beehive construction, as introduced by the Normans. The birds enter through a hole in the top, while the four bands of slate around the structure prevent predatory rats scrambling up the outside. *(Author's collection)*

The architectural pigeon towers at Isfahan in Iran, the contents of which have greened the surrounding arid plains for centuries. (© *Jerry Harpur*)

The eighth circle of Dante's Inferno, as illustrated by Botticelli. From the bridge Virgil points out the courtesan Tais scratching her head which is smeared with excrement; she is surrounded by groaning, snorting, hand-clapping flatterers wallowing in pools of excrement. He called it Malebolge (or Evil Pockets) because of its structure, described as a grey stony place between a rockface above and a deep well below. Grey and earthy black-brown colours traditionally represent baser things, ranks and attitudes. (© Bildarchiv Preußischer Kulturbesitz, Berlin)

Stinking, foetid, inhuman conditions faced the 'slaves' employed to dig guano on the Chincha Islands. The parallels between the reality of this nineteenth-century engraving and the worst imaginings of Dante and Botticelli in depicting Hell are striking. (© Mary Evans Picture Library)

A portrait of the hero. Two flightless dung beetles hard at work in the Addo Elephant National Park, South Africa. *(Anthony Bannister)*

A stockpile of dung fuel near Rajmahal in India. Such fuel is essential in areas where wood is scarce. *(© Erica Hunningher)*

Nursery humour on an adult chamber-pot 'To the wife Keep me close I will not tell A present'. Variants included a watching eye or busts of disliked figures such as Gladstone or Napoleon. During the Second World War this was revived with likenesses of Hitler. *(© Sothebys)*

The luxurious choice of hot, warm, cold, dry or steam, plus latrines, were housed within the baths at Chesters Roman Fort in Northumberland. Smooth wooden seats were suspended over the latrine channel in the foreground; the niches in the background in the changing-room probably held statues for each day of the week. *(Author's collection)*

The necessary house at the Governor's Palace in Williamsburg was built out of sight at the bottom of the ballroom garden – but handily at the corner of the walled kitchen garden. At the base of the pit below the seat was a sand-filled tray that could be slid out and its contents put to good use. *(Author's collection)*

Home, home on the plain – out on America's Midwest plains independence is hard won by Ada McColl as she pushes her wheelbarrow stacked with buffalo chips for fuel. The little girl's immaculately white-dressed dolly provides a contrasting whiff of comfort.
(© Bettmann/CORBIS)

The necessary house at George Washington's former home, Mount Vernon, was placed at the corner of the walled garden and was well shaded to keep it cool and discreet. (Author's collection)

Fox dung gleaming in the morning sun within the walled garden of Edzell Castle. (© *Pat Crocker Riversong Herbals*)

This carved snuff box of about 1840 depicts a squatting man and explicitly includes his dung as a third support. (© *www.boxes.co.uk*)

into heaps. Anyone who had borrowed a load of straw had to re-pay the loan with a load of farmyard manure (FYM). After matur-ing for a few months the muck heaps were carted out in tumbrils to fertilise the fields. Labourers would unload it with a special tool, the muck chrome, which had a long handle and long tines specially adapted for raking out FYM. Snelling recorded that the richest manure was produced by fattening cattle or pigs and the poorest from milking herds, their milk having absorbed all the calcium and phosphates.

Early eighteenth-century readers could feel the link between God and gentlemen when they turned to *Le Jardinier Solitaire*, subtitled *Dialogues between a Gentleman and a Gard'ner*. The author, a Carthusian monk, wrote in catechism style. (I assume, as Carthusians lived as hermits within a community, the written word was a permitted method of communication.) The dialogue of Chapter XXIII concludes by advising the gentleman to discern the heat of his raised dunged seedbeds by putting his finger into it. Keen to further his knowledge and to bring us back to straws:

> *Gent*: It comes into my Mind to ask you how to make Hot Beds for Mushrooms; after that I shall have Reason to be satisfy'd with all your Instructions concerning the Manner of making my Fruit and Kitchin Garden.
>
> *Chap.* XXIV The Manner and Time of making Hot Beds for Mush-rooms. Gard. Begin by laying in a Provision of Dung of Wheat-Straw,

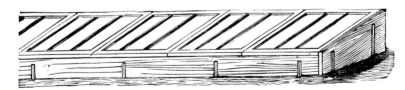

Sam Beeton illustrated this long frame with further advice: 'In covering the lights of a hotbed during frosts or rough winds it is advisable to avoid letting the mats, or whatnot, hang over the sides as there is often the danger of conducting rank steam from the linings into the frame.' He also suggested piling the dung 'nearly up to the glass to allow for sinking'.

and never of Rye. . . . 'Twill be necessary to mix the Dung well together, that is to say, the Excrementitious Balls with the Straw.

Had the monk noted that wheat straw was cleaner and more absorbent, so better meeting the well-drained but moisture-retentive requirements of mushrooms? He suggests topping up with 'long [i.e. hot] dung' and watering with 'Water in which the Peels, Stalks and Refuge of Mushrooms have been newly boyl'd, pour'd on hot, is best'. The Gentleman is guaranteed 'good and large Mushrooms at little expence'.

Two hundred years later in France Claude Monet's garden at Giverny was (and still is) an impressionist showcase and inspiration, as was his dining table during his lifetime. Elsewhere in Giverny he owned the Maison Bleue, where he and his gardeners raised a variety of mushrooms with no expense spared.

Mr Sam Beeton (husband of cookery queen Mrs Beeton and tireless publisher) wrote *Beeton's Shilling Gardener* and, later, *Everyday Gardening*, both of which include sections on manure and guano. He wrote: 'The excreta of most animals are too rank and strong for flower-garden purposes, applied in a pure state; by mixing, however, it will be . . . much more valuable . . . among these With's "Improved Universal Carbon Manure" to be obtained from the Hereford Society for Aiding the Industrious.'

Hall, in his *Fertilizers and Manures*, devoted a chapter to the 'Composition of Farmyard Manure', reporting an array of experiments with horses, sheep and bullocks penned in a variety of stables and enclosures with different litters, with due regard paid to flooring, cleaning and feeding. Bullocks were fed either on hay and roots or on a fattening ration of cake with hay and roots, and in 1907 their dung was sampled as it left the yard. Both lots contained virtually equal amounts of insoluble nitrogen but the cake-fed end product contained a staggering three times as much ammonia. This created high excitement as it was tilled just once into four-year rotation fields of swede, barley, mangolds and wheat: the results showed an 83 per cent increase in yield in the first year, a rise which was maintained in years two and three with increases of 37 per cent and 18 per cent respectively from the cake-fed dung. Hall sang the praises of the extremely lasting character of nitrogenous compounds in farmyard manure, quoting experiments carried out in the fields around the Rothamsted Experimental Station near St Albans, starting in 1856. For eight years, from 1856 to 1864, 14 tons of dung per

Percentages of certain Constituents of Litter.			
	Nitrogen.	Phosphoric Acid.	Potash.
Wheat straw, ...	0·48	0·23	0·49
Barley straw, ...	0·48	0·19	0·93
Oat straw, ...	0·40	0·28	0·97
Pea haulm, ...	1·04	0·38	1·07
Potato haulm, ...	0·50	0·10	0·30
Heather,...	0·90	0·10	0·40
Fern, ...	2·40	0·45	2·42
Rushes, ...	0·40	0·35	1·67
Beech-tree leaves, ...	0·80	0·24	0·30
Peat, ...	1·50	trace.	0·10

The type and quantity of litter used for the bedding of animals has a major influence on the value of the resulting manure for the garden. The table from *Thompson's Gardener's Assistant*, 1900, shows the amount of the most valuable constituents in certain materials commonly used as litter for farm animals.

	Water.	Organic Matter.	Nitrogen.	Phosphoric Acid.	Potash.	Lime.	Magnesia.
Fresh human fæces,	77·2	19·8	1·0	1·10	0·25	0·62	0·36
Fresh human urine,	96·3	2·4	0·6	0·17	0·20	0·02	0·02
Mixture of the two,	93·5	5·1	0·7	0·26	0·21	0·09	0·06

Wolff's table from *Thompson's Gardener's Assistant*, 1900. His 'night-soil analysis' shows that fresh human excrement is richer in 'fertilising matters' than that of farm animals.

acre were applied every year to one grass plot, while the other was left unmanured. No manure was then added to either plot but some forty years later the manured plot still produced higher yields. Not only was the soil richer but its texture and water-retaining qualities were greatly superior.

Like many such bodies, the Museum of Garden History in London acts as a storehouse of history in concrete, visual, written and oral form. One retired gardener remembered his years as a garden boy before the Second World War, recalling his life in the bothy and the chores: 'One single-handed job was to collect sheep

Sheep droppings create an intricate pattern across the landscape, often providing trails for autumn mushrooms.

and cow manure from the fields of one of the estate farms (not a job taught at college!). Secured in hessian sacks, the fruits of my labour were immersed in large water tanks and after some dunking and stirring the resulting liquid was used as liquid feed for various plants. Sweet peas especially benefited from regular watering with the sheep concoction!' Collecting cowpats would be relatively straightforward but as sheep do not drink much they produce hundreds of little round droppings. Anyone who has walked across sheep fields knows it is almost impossible not to tread in them. Imagine having to collect them!

The Last Straw

Are you troubled with warts? Then take yourself to the nearest dung-heap. The Revd Hilderic Friend recorded an Irish remedy: 'Find a straw with nine knees, and cut the knots that form the joints of every one of them (if there are any more knots throw them away); then bury the knots in a midden or dung-heap; as the joints rot so will the warts.' He helpfully added that the straw of wheat, oats or barley are equally efficacious. Friend then quoted Francis Bacon: 'They say the like is done by rubbing of warts with a green Elder stick, and then burying the stick to rot in muck.'

The Great Aussie Salute

In the nineteenth century all land in Australia was deemed as being the property of the Crown. Pioneers and colonists arriving from Europe selected their piece of land and then paid the Crown for the right to farm it. In principle, towns were founded at 60-mile intervals, providing every farming family with a centre with markets, schools, stores and churches within a 30-mile horse or buggy ride. Vast sheep paddocks and cattle pastures were established and soon they were littered with soft dung that attracted swarms of flies. The indigenous kangaroo and wallaby population

Australian dung beetles are adept at clearing up the dry pellets of kangaroos and wallabies. 'Roo-poo' is now being used to manufacture a textured paper.

did not create this problem as a native dung beetle had evolved alongside them whose lifecycle worked around their dry pellets. The Aussie Salute involves swatting away the flies buzzing around your face before you speak.

This is a story in two parts, stemming from a small town founded during the 1850s Gold Rush. Cootaburra stands on the banks of the Corella river in western New South Wales and today it is surrounded with wheat fields, sheep paddocks and cattle. Herds of cattle were introduced in the nineteenth century, and as they grazed they produced the customary ten pats a day. These were soft, wet, large and too big for the native dung beetles to handle so they simply ignored them, leaving the way open for flies, which arrived in droves and bred in millions. Sometimes it reached the point where there were so many flies that even breathing was difficult – until 1967, when biologists introduced African dung beetles. One Australian farmer working over a million acres in the countryside beyond Perth at this time claimed his best wedding present was large numbers of African dung beetles. Even better is that their introduction seems not to have had a deleterious effect on the native beetle population. Henri Fabre would doubtless have been proud of their stercoracious work.

Penning Portent

There are parallels to the Australian experience in Kenya, where curiously the amount of savannah forage rises with higher numbers of indigenous wildlife and drops with lesser numbers of livestock. From 1982 Ingeburg Burchard has undertaken research to compare the outcomes of grazing and dunging by these two groups. Much of her research has centred on the Nairobi National Park where in the last thirty years livestock numbers have dropped but they have been replaced by three-and-a-half times more wildlife. Evaporation exceeds precipitation in the African savannahs so the soils are dry and mostly alkaline, but their resident populations ensure ready-made organic fertilisers. Burchard noted that the water and microbes in the digestive systems of the wild herbivores created a beneficial cycle – they graze, digest and excrete the plants as dung. The excreta is cleared by dung beetles and insects, whose own dung then creates a prepared fertiliser for the plants. Although the flocks of domestic animals such as cattle, goats, sheep and camels eat just as much grass, they excrete less dung, over half of which is in their night enclosures and never recycled – some of these middens can remain for years and years. Most of the dung on the pastures is left by the dung beetles and termites, and what remains dries out to become a nitrogen-rich feed. Good news you might think, but actually it's not. In fact, it lowers the diversity of the grasses that grow and these richer pastures are indigestible to local herbivores.

The ecological damage continues in the form of methane pollution. Wild animals break down their dietary cellulose during chewing (rather than by the anaerobic method of ruminants), so they void only negligible amounts of methane. In contrast, the figures for livestock make you want to grab an oxygen mask: 1,000 cattle produce 815g of methane daily, and 1,000 goats at least 470g, while the more polite local society of 1,000 wildebeest produce a mere 12g and 1,000 giraffes 100g. In addition, Burchard noted that African savannah grasses use atmospheric nitrogen nearly exclusively. If you set the above figures against the (useful) dung produced each day by guests versus locals, a cow excretes 4g dry matter dung per kilogram body weight while a buffalo provides a generous 15g, and sheep and goats a miserly 3g compared with a Thompson gazelle's 18g. In terms of grazing, local wildlife nibble selectively, but introduced livestock are greedy

Bewick's excellent 1792 engraving of the giraffe, or cameleopard, is accompanied by this description: 'It leads a solitary life far from the habitations of men; for whose use it is rendered unfit, by the enormous disproportion of its parts.' More than 200 years later it contributes to Zoo poo and the hardened dung is used to make jewellery.

grubbers that weaken or uproot the grasses as they graze relentlessly. As the grasses die out, their roots can no longer retain any of the precious water that is available, nor slow down surface run-off. In conclusion, to quote Burchard:

> It is beyond any doubt that African wild animals are the most important and indispensable part of the decomposition process. Protection and restoration of the full spectrum of game animals as well as protection and restoration of their environment have to be given priority all over Africa. If wildlife has gone it never comes back . . . Nature never compromises, it reacts.

Hot Dung

In Johnson's definition of excrement – 'That which is thrown out as useless, noxious, or corrupted from the natural passages of the body' – he quotes *Arbuthnot on Ailments*: 'The excrements of horses are nothing but hay, and, as such, combustible.' Compostable for hot beds perhaps, but not for warming fires. But throughout the world dried dung has been used as a fuel. Celia Fiennes, travelling through England in 1698, noted:

> There was no gates to Peterborough town, and as I pass'd the road I saw upon the walls of the ordinary peoples houses and walls of their out houses the cown dung plaister'd up to drie in cakes which they use for fireing – its a very offensive fewell but the country people use little else in these parts.

It is a source of fuel that is still actively used in many barren lands, especially where wood is scarce. Two of the photographs in this book illustrate the use of dung as a fuel in India: the colour plate of a stockpile near Rajmahal and, on the cover, a young girl from Rajasthan carrying dried patties of cow dung on her head.

5

STABLE FARE

Dung. Under this title our attention must be confined to the faeces
and urines of animals, and that one most common compound,
stable dung.

George Johnson, The Cottage Gardener *(1852)*

Forking Out

Mucking out stables is perhaps most famously associated with
Hercules's labour to clean out the thirty-year accumulation of
cattle dung for King Augeas by diverting rivers. But when tackling
such tasks logic is as important as muscle. In the old Norse tale
The Mastermaid a prince agrees to clean three stables in order to
win the hand of a giant's daughter. Armed with a pitch-fork he
starts the job, but for every forkload he tosses, ten times the
amount of dung returns. The princess advises him to turn the
pitch-fork upside down and just use the handle – and it works.

The use of horse dung can be dated back to the discovery of
oats and horses in Tartary and their introduction into Egypt in the
third millennium BC. Much later, in 1607 John Norden noted:
'The soyle of the stables of London, especially neere the Thames
side, is carried Westward by water, to Chelsey, Fulham, Battersey,
Putney, and those parts for their sandie grounds.' In the late nineteenth century fears were voiced that London would be soon lost
under 9ft of horse manure as supply far outstripped demand. One
way to use up the surplus would be to try the following anonymous recipe for 'horse dung water, for Agues and feavers and all

The common cart-horse, as illustrated by Thomas Bewick, was used as a packhorse to deliver goods into cities and bring back dung for the fields, as well as leaving dungy offerings of its own on the city streets for domestic gardeners to collect.

distempers'. It instructs the reader: 'Take horse dunge and put to it so much Ale as will make it like hasty puding, and put it into your still. Then putt on ye topp one pound of treakell, and a quarter of a pound of genger in powder and the same in sweet anisseeds, and so distill all these together.' It closes with the suggestion that 'this water is good for women in labour and in childbed'. (Presumably after the camel dung contraceptive pessary had failed.) This must rate alongside the belief that kissing a horse's anus prevents chapped lips and mandrakes emit fatal shrieks against the person who pulls them from the earth. John Gerard's splenetic words on mandrakes can be equally applied: 'There hath beene many ridiculous tales brought up of this plant, whether of old wives, or some runnagate Surgeons or Physicke-mongers I know not . . . henceforth cast out of your bookes and memory; knowing this, that they are all and everie part of them false and most untrue.'

Dung features heavily in the works of Gerard and Hyll, writing just twenty years apart. The latter provides very precise instructions about what to do with it:

In the midst of April, or in the beginning of May (as the Moon shall happen to be in the wane) dig a ditch about a yard deep, and lay some three quarters of a yard of Horse dung therein; then cover the dung over a foot thick with good earth, laying your seeds along on the earth dry, and cover them an inch thick with light earth, and every night (until May be past) cover them with a wet cloth or straw, to keep away the frost. . . . And note, that when the Cucumber hath three leaves, you may then remove them to other places. The Pumpion seeds should be set a finger deep in the earth; and the Cabbadges should be removed when they are a handfull high.

Horse Play

After the death of Jean-Baptiste de la Quintinye the *potager du roi* at Versailles continued to provide early and out-of-season fruit and vegetables under the supervision of the capable François le Normand. But while its importance was knocked by the creation of a royal botanic garden for Louis XV in the Trianon at Versailles, the worst blow resulted from a major disagreement between the potager and the 'palefreniers' (ostlers or grooms). All donations of horse dung ceased for thirty years, leaving le Normand with the task of setting up his own dung-sourcing business. A few decades later on the other side of the Atlantic 'the greatest natural botanist' John Bartram used a potent horse dung brew to produce bumper crops of hay that far outstripped the yields of all his eighteenth-century Pennsylvanian neighbours. Never one to waste anything, he used ox bladders to wrap up the roots and shoots he dispatched to Europe. During the 1990s the mucking-out of the Birmingham police stables 'helped' in the restoration of the 1730s gardens at Castle Bromwich.

Gertrude Jekyll revealed the secret of her successful rhododendrons at Munstead Wood near Godalming in *Home and Garden*. She bought the 15 acres in 1883 and lived there for nearly 50 years. Undeterred by the sandy, heathy soil, she dug a trench 2ft deep around each plant and filled it with a 'good' barrowload of peaty topsoil. Just out of the new roots' reach was placed a good dressing of cow manure, a treat that the plants had to work for. Each rhododendron was surrounded by a shallow depression to direct all available water to the roots. Lastly each rhododendron received a liberal coating of cow manure every year. In her writings and her nursery, however, Jekyll never forgot the plight of town gardeners or empire-builders creating temporary gardens. She looked no further for inspiration than the poor sandy soils of nearby Aldershot with its large mobile military population. How fortunate were the gardeners here to have easy access to vast supplies of stable manure. Although it lacked the cooling quality of cow manure and the richness of pig, she commented, consideration should be given to its nourishing nature and precious chemical constituents. Dig deep and mulch more, was her advice, especially with 'long' stable litter. ('Long' has decayed and is protective, while 'short' is hot and nutritious.)

In the late nineteenth century my great-grandfather and his three brothers ran a branch of the family shipping business from Hamburg. At the outbreak of the First World War my grandfather was still at school there but was immediately banned as an English citizen. His father and uncles were quickly interned, followed by my grandfather when he reached 16, in the British prison camp at Ruhleben, formerly Berlin's trotting racecourse. The accommodation was dire, with 6 men to a horsebox and some 365 men living in stables designed for just 7 horses, parts of which were still full of dung. Military latrines dug for the interns about a quarter of a mile away were described by the American ambassador as not only a health hazard to the camp but to Berlin as well. In the midst of the mire and stygian gloom the 4,000 prisoners organised various improvements, among the first of which was the introduction of small and modest gardens beneath the windows of some of the barracks. Barrack VIII, for example, had a rose garden. The interns even created a Horticultural Society, which was later affiliated to the Royal Horticultural Society in London. By 1917 negotiations were under way to convert the unused half of the racecourse into a kitchen garden, and by the end of the year fresh vegetables were being supplied to their canteen. The Germans asked for fifteen red

Green and scented camouflage became a possibility in the Ruhleben camp thanks to copious horse manure.

cabbages to be delivered to their officers' mess and for all outer leaves to be supplied as cattle fodder. As the seed was provided for the benefit of the interned, the first request was refused but it was agreed that the outer leaves could be supplied to the Germans in exchange for cattle manure. This helped to produce quality melons, tomatoes, cut flowers and sweet peas for the Ruhleben Horticultural Society flower shows.

Drop In, Pick Up

Whatever their final destination, the collection and removal of horse droppings from stables and pastures is straightforward good husbandry. Left in the field, the droppings provide shelter for procreating parasitic tapeworms and roundworms, the resultant eggs migrating through the protective dung on to the ground. When the little worms hatch they are picked up by grazing horses, and the cycle begins again. Worse, many worm species have now become immune to deworming drugs. Thus droppings need to be collected on a daily basis, a routine job undertaken by hardworking stable staff. But no longer! A splendid mechanical beast, 'The Predator', manufactured not far from Newmarket in Suffolk, offers a vacuuming system for stable and fields. (Amusingly, its top of the range model is called the Jumbo.) The droppings of horses, as well as those of alpacas and llamas, are simply sucked up through hoses running between something that looks like a quad-bike and a standard hopper-shaped trailer. There is even a blow adaptor so that you can revacuum the droppings and blow them into a skip or on to the compost heap.

There are other ways to give your soil a head start. Watching and abiding by the phases of the moon is an ancient way of improving yields. The head gardener of the Tresillian Estate near Newquay, R.J. Harris, has set up a gloriously illustrative website on moon gardening, at www.moongardening.fsnet.co.uk. Harris has also been instrumental in setting up the National Manure Database, where browsers can access not only a bountiful picture show but also a list of farms, stables and riding schools with a surplus of horse manure. Head to London and the West Country with a shovel and its yours for the taking!

> There once was a horse from Cape Verdes,
> Who produced most unusual turds,
> By the simplest means
> He'd eat corn and beans
> And make succotash for the birds.

Sound and Fury

Wu Ching Tsung Yao's treatise on military techniques in China, completed in 1044, provides the first record of the explosive and pyrotechnic uses of saltpetre. Saltpetre – potassium nitrate – was imported into Europe from India during the Middle Ages until a source was found nearer home. Stables and outbuildings built of and housing earth and manure sprouted an efflorescence when regularly in contact with urine. These deposits were carefully scraped off for their saltpetre content, which was a crucial element of gunpowder. According to the records, it was at the Battle of Crecy in 1346 that English soldiers used gunpowder for the first time.

In order to ensure an independent supply Queen Elizabeth's Privy Council paid £300 to a Friesian refugee, Gerhard Honrick, to reveal how saltpetre could be manufactured. His reply? First source your ingredients: 'Fyrst black earth the blacker the better. The next is Urine, namely of those persons which drink either wyne or strong bears. Then Dong specially of those horses, which be fed with ootes, and be always kept in the stables. The fourth is Lyme made of plaster of Parys. The Lyme which is made of Oyster Shellis is the best. . . .' All these items were formed into a heap which was regularly turned until sufficient potassium nitrate salts had formed.

There was a worrying shortfall of gunpowder in 1588 at the time of the threat from the Spanish Armada, so from 1589 manufacturers were licensed by royal letters patent. John Evelyn's forebears achieved increasing prominence as holders of these appointments, which Evelyn himself continued in the 1660s.

However, it now became increasingly difficult to maintain sufficient supplies of manure, and as a consequence 'saltpetre men' were appointed, who had the right to enter any stables or dovecotes and dig up what was required. James I introduced a system of weekly quotas and in 1625 Charles I decreed that all dovecotes should have 'good and mellow' earth floors instead of paving. Unnecessary damage was often done to these buildings by the saltpetre men, much to the grievance of their owners. One such was Christopher Wren's father, whose claim for compensation against the saltpetre men still exists in the Public Record Office. Dated 1636, it accuses 'Thomas Thornhill, Salt Peter Man', of 'undermining and throwing downe the Pidgeon House of the said Rectory'. Wren had suffered the same sort of vandalism eight years earlier.

Well Versed

In 1785 William Cowper published a long poem on rural themes,
The Task, in which stable fare assumes the role of hero. 'The
Garden' is the third book of the six, and as you read it you get a
sense of Cowper as an evangelical revivalist and precursor to
William Wordsworth. This chapter finishes with a lengthy quotation from the poem, which does not lend itself to short extracts,
so relax and take an eighteenth-century saunter through the
cycles of the soil and its potential bounty:

> To raise the prickly and green-coated gourd,
> So grateful to the palate, and when rare
> So coveted, else base and disesteem'd –
> Food for the vulgar merely – is an art
> That toiling ages have but just matured,
> And at this moment unassay'd in song.
> Yet gnats have had, and frogs and mice, long since,
> Their eulogy; those sang the Mantuan bard,
> And these the Grecian, in ennobling strains;
> And in thy numbers, Phillips, shines for aye
> The solitary shilling. Pardon then,
> Ye sage dispensers of poetic fame,
> The ambition of one meaner far, whose powers,
> Presuming an attempt not less sublime,
> Pant for the praise of dressing to the taste
> Of critic appetite, no sordid fare,
> A cucumber, while costly yet and scarce.
>
> The stable yields a stercoraceous heap,
> Impregnated with quick fermenting salts,
> And potent to resist the freezing blast:
> For, ere the beech and elm have cast their leaf
> Deciduous, when now November dark
> Checks vegetation in the torpid plant
> Exposed to his cold breath, the task begins.

Warily therefore, and with prudent heed,
He seeks a favour'd spot; that where he builds
The agglomerated pile his frame may front
The sun's meridian disk, and at the back
Enjoy close shelter, wall, or reeds, or hedge
Impervious to the wind. First he bids spread
Dry fern or litter'd hay, that may imbibe
The ascending damps; then leisurely impose,
And lightly, shaking it with agile hand
From the full fork, the saturated straw.
What longest binds the closest forms secure
The shapely side, that as it rises takes,
By just degrees, an overhanging breadth,
Sheltering the base with its projected eaves;
The uplifted frame, compact at every joint,
And overlaid with clear translucent glass,
He settles next upon the sloping mount,
Whose sharp declivity shoots off secure
From the dash'd pane the deluge as it falls.
He shuts it close, and the first labour ends.
Thrice must the voluble and restless Earth
Spin round upon her axle, ere the warmth,
Slow gathering in the midst, through the square mass
Diffused, attain the surface: when, behold!
A pestilent and most corrosive steam,
Like a gross fog Boeotian, rising fast,
And fast condensed upon the dewy sash,
Asks egress; which obtain'd, the overcharged
And drench'd conservatory breathes abroad,
In volumes wheeling slow, the vapour dank;
And, purified, rejoices to have lost
Its foul inhabitant. But to assuage
The impatient fervour, which it first conceives
Within its reeking bosom, threatening death
to his young hopes, requires discreet delay.
Experience, slow preceptress, teaching oft

The way to glory by miscarriage foul,
Must prompt him, and admonish how to catch
The auspicious moment, when the temper'd heat,
Friendly to vital motion, may afford
Soft fomentation, and invite the seed.
The seed, selected wisely, plump, and smooth,
And glossy, he commits to pots of size
Diminutive, well fill'd with well-prepared
And fruitful soil, that has been treasured long,
And drank no moisture from the dripping clouds.
These on the warm and genial earth, that hides
The smoking manure, and o'erspreads it all,
He places lightly, and, as time subdues
The rage of fermentation, plunges deep
In the soft medium, till they stand immersed.
Then rise the tender germs, upstarting quick,
And spreading wide their spongy lobes; at first
Pale, wan, and livid; but assuming soon,
If fann'd by balmy and nutritious air,
Strain'd through the friendly mats, a vivid green.
Two leaves produced, two rough indented leaves,
Cautious he pinches from the second stalk
A pimple, that portends a future sprout,
And interdicts its growth. Thence straight succeed
The branches, sturdy to his utmost wish;
Prolific all, and harbingers of more.
The crowded roots demand enlargement now,
And transplantation in an ampler space.
Indulged in what they wish, they soon supply
Large foliage, o'ershadowing golden flowers,
Blown on the summit of the apparent fruit,
These have their sexes! and when summer shines,
The bee transports the fertilising meal
From flower to flower, and e'en the breathing air
Wafts the rich prize to its appointed use.
Not so when winter scowls. Assistant Art

Then acts in Nature's office, brings to pass
The glad espousals, and ensures the crop.
Grudge not, ye rich (since Luxury must have
His dainties, and the World's more numerous half
Lives by contriving delicates for you)
Grudge not the cost. Ye little know the cares,
The vigilance, the labour, and the skill,
That day and night are exercised, and hang
Upon the ticklish balance of suspense,
That ye may garnish your profuse regales
With summer fruits brought forth by wintry suns.
Ten thousand dangers lie in wait to thwart
The process. heat and cold, and wind, and steam,
Moisture and drought, mice, worms, and swarming flies,
Minute as dust, and numberless, oft work
Dire disappointment, that admits no cure
And which no care can obviate. It were long,
Too long, to tell the expedients and the shifts,
Which he that fights a season so severe
Devises, while he guards his tender trust;
And oft at last in vain. The learn'd and wise
Sarcastic would exclaim, and judge the song
Cold as its theme, and like its theme the fruit
Of too much labour, worthless when produced.

Today the wise will tell vegetable gardeners that if they tot up all the costs of the manurance involved it is cheaper to buy fruit and vegetables, but for most, taste and health and pride far outweigh any monetary expenditure.

6

FERTILE FLIGHTS AND FOWL FANCIES

> There once was a lady named Muire,
> Whose mind was so frightfully pure
> That she fainted away
> At a friend's house one day
> When she saw some canary manure.

Bottoms Up

The anatomy of a bird is such that it urinates and defecates from the same orifice, resulting in a more colourful deposit, as delicately expressed by Francis Bacon: 'The excrementious moisture passeth in birds through a fairer and more delicate strainer than in beasts.' Anyone living in the vicinity of berry-eating birds would recognise, for example, the post-elderberry deep purples, while the urine can be detected as white, pasty splotches. It is another of nature's tricks. The berries on many northern shrubs and trees, such as hawthorn, do not colour up until the seeds are ready to be dispersed – ideally via an avian digestive system. (While on the subject of colour, we should note that when blue whales eat pink shrimp – at a ton per mouthful – they defecate giant blobs of what looks like strawberry ice-cream, some 10in wide and several yards long, into the sea.)

Birds drop away from the nest, and even their offspring have well-trained digestive systems. Newly hatched chicks, whose eager beaks can be seen demanding food from exhausted parents, reverse the process by hanging their rear ends over the side of the nest. Just watch the entrance to a house martin's carefully constructed nest for a demonstration of the beak/bottom routine – and spot the evidence all down the walls. Many other chicks produce a neat dropping with a coating like a bag, which the parents dutifully collect and drop elsewhere to keep predators off their trail.

The chicken and egg paradox is perfectly illustrated by mistletoe, which nestles in the trunks of oak and apple trees as well as hawthorns, maples, Abies and Euphorbia. In the Dark Ages its parasitic, elevated growth represented sacred power, the Druids harvesting it with a golden sickle while two white bulls were sacrificed. The branches were not allowed to touch the ground, but the berries – bringers of good luck and fecundity – were harvested and distributed as a protection from spirits. Among birds, thrushes, blackbirds and robins particularly delight in the mistletoe's white berries, but the seeds are very sticky. Once again, the wiles of nature provide the perfect sowing and germination cycle for the plant, as the birds have to wipe their bottoms energetically against the rough bark to dislodge the seeds. Thus the seeds are 'delivered' into the furrows and crevices in the tree's bark where they can take root.

There are a number of deeply rooted superstitions concerning mistletoe. If you should dream of mistletoe, for example, you should take it as a warning to be cautious in love. Geoffrey Grigson, in *The Englishman's Flora*, records that in Worcestershire a bough of mistletoe was given to the first cow to calve after New Year's Day, in the belief that this would avert ill-luck for the whole dairy. Another such superstition ties in neatly with some Scottish dung folklore. In Scotland the cow's dung was forced into her calf's mouth before it took its first suck, to protect it from witches and fairies.

The Roman writer Columella favoured pigeon dung, followed by that of hen and other fowls, but never that of water fowl, which he deemed too cold. Varro praised blackbird dung as vastly improving forage crops for oxen and swine, presumably after they had feasted on his fruit crop! In Rome young men chewed light bread to feed to pigeons to improve their flesh for the table – and presumably

Fertile flight and flightless birds are depicted in biblical lands in this Victorian illustrated children's Bible, with most of the dung references carefully reworded or omitted altogether. The reference to dove's dung being eaten during the great famine of Samaria refers not to dung but to the bulb *Ornithogalum umbellatum*.

resulting in anaemic droppings. From the palatial park to the tiny courtyard, many Roman gardens contained bird cages or aviaries providing sound, colour and fertility. The farmyard population, the source of varied and fertile dung, historically included the dung-cock (also a nickname for medieval cowards), dung-fowl and dung-hen, so named to distinguish them from the pleasures of bagging superior wild game. They also serve the dual purpose of pecking up predatory insects and caterpillars while gently fertilising the ground. One Roman proverb – 'Every cock will crow upon his own dunghill' – was widely used in medieval England, Chaucer's delightful story of Chanticleer being a charming example.

Dung Dreaming

The language of flowers and the meaning of dreams enjoyed a popular revival in the nineteenth century, with one Victorian source warning that dreaming of dung or dirt signifies sickness and dishonour. Dreaming that you were falling into it warned that you would be treacherously dealt with. Chaucer's *The Nun's Priest's Tale* opens with the happy throng in the poor widow's yard, three sows and a cock called Chanticleer 'who was master in some measure of seven hens, all there to do his pleasure'. The gracious Lady Pertelote was his loveliest first lady and one night she was disturbed by Chanticleer's groaning and starting. He had had a dreadful dream about being kidnapped by a sort of hound, 'a blend of yellow and red, His ears and tail were tipped with sable fur . . . a russet cur'. Pertelote dismissed his fearful dream and put it down to constipation:

> Worms for a day or two I'll have to give
> As a digestive, then your laxative.
> Centaury, fumitory, caper-spurge
> And hellebore will make a splendid purge;
> And then there's laurel or the blackthorn berry,
> Ground-ivy too that makes our yard so merry . . .

All these were equally used traditionally as human laxatives, but Chanticleer was convinced that dreams could be portents of disaster and he recounted the tragic story of two men on a pilgrimage who separated in their search for overnight shelter. One settled down for the night beside some oxen and a plough, but soon started to dream of his comrade, not once but three times, calling for help, saying that he was slain and asking his friend to go to the west gate of the town, where he would find a cart loaded with dung:

> And in that dung my body had been hidden.
> Boldly arrest that cart as you are bidden.
> It was my money that they killed me for . . .

The friend went first to the innkeeper, who said his friend had left at dawn, but when he raced to the west gate he found there a cart loaded with dung – with his friend's body in the middle.

> All the town officers in great confusion
> Seized on the carter and they gave him hell,
> And then they racked the innkeeper as well,
> And both confessed . . .

Fox dung contains the fur, feathers and bones of his prey and has a particularly foul smell described as musty with a touch of old socks. You may not see him, but you will know where he's been.

Note the pigeon towers in this view of Isfahan. Pigeons were legion and there were no fewer than three thousand towers, built according to Chardin 'less to house the pigeons than to gather the birds' droppings'. These were especially prized for melon fields.

Side by side on their perch, his bad dream forgotten, Chanticleer praised the sensation of Pertelote's feathery touch and later, safe on the ground, 'feathered her in wanton play'. Cock of the dung-hill gloriously arrayed, he was almost immediately snapped up by flattering words into the jaws of a local fox. Turning compliment to his own advantage, he extricated himself by beguiling the fox into opening his boastful mouth. The moral of the story is that you should listen to your dreams and be on guard against flattery.

Billing and Cooing

The King James translation of the Old Testament recounts how, during the siege of Samaria and the ensuing famine, even an ass's head 'and the fourth part of a cab of dove's dung [was sold] for four-score pieces of silver'. Dove's dung requires the presence of the dove itself, and there is no doubt that had such birds been present then the Samarians would soon have been forced to eat them. In fact, dove's dung is the common name for the bulb

Ornithogalum umbellatum, better known today by its common name, Star of Bethlehem. These plants naturalise over arid hillsides and when they flower the ground appears littered with white splotches – hence their other common name. The Latin name translates as birds' milk, and in the Middle East the bulbs were dried and ground into powder which was then mixed with flour. The English herbalist John Parkinson, apothecary to Charles I's queen Henrietta Maria, described it as 'sweeter in taste to any chestnut and serving as well for a necessary need as for delight'.

There is evidence of simple doocots at Skara Brae that date back 5,000 years, while the earliest doocotes in Scotland were in caves. Dovecotes and pigeon houses remained an important part of the rural economy – providing both protein and dung – until the introduction of large-scale turnip growing which enabled the overwintering of livestock – providing, again, both protein and dung. In the sixteenth century readers of Thomas Tusser were given a monthly abstract. January's included advice on doves:

> Feed Doves, but kill not,
> if loose them ye will not.
> Dove house repaire,
> make Dovehole faire.
> For hop ground cold,
> Dove doong woorth gold.

Tusser also advised shifting all types of dung when frost was on the ground so that the carts did not sink into the mud. In general, the droppings from pigeon houses and dovecotes were removed in the winter when the birds were not nesting, and it was often used on the furthest fields as it was reckoned to be ten times more effective than that from cattle and sheep. Thus achieving maximum fertilisation for minimum transportation – early time and motion?

Identifying methods for improving the soil's yield dominates early agricultural and horticultural writings. We need look no further than Tusser's near-contemporary Thomas Hyll's *The*

A modern dovecote in The Alnwick Garden provides some dung as well as sound and movement in the upper walled garden.

Gardeners' Labyrinth. Chapter Ten is entitled: 'Of kindes of dung, and which is well commended for the dunging of Gardens'.

As touching the worthinesse and excellency of dung, the Greek writers of Husbandry (to whom many of the Latin Authors consent) affirm that the Doves dung is the best, because the same possesseth a mighty hotnesse, for which they willed this dung to be strawed the thinner, and in a manner (as thin to be scattered abroad) as seeds on the earth, whereby the same may so season the earth measurably, and not on a heap or thick bestowed (as Mr Varro reporteth) much like to

Interior of ruined dovecote in Brittany showing nesting sites with ledges to prevent rats from running up the inside.

the dung of Cattel thrown abroad on the ground. The dung also of the Hen and other fowls greatly commended for the sourenes, except the dung of Geese, Ducks, and other water fowls, for their much and thin dunging. And although this dung at last, be weaker than the others, yet may the same profitable, as the selfe same Varro witnesseth out of the Greek instructions of Husbandry. A commendation next is attributed to the Asses dung, in that the same beast for his leisurely eating digesteth easier, and causeth the better dung, which bestowed in the earth, for that the same is most fertile by nature, bringeth or yeeldeth forth least store of weeds, and procureth very much all plants and hearbs: yes, this causeth the most sweet and pleasantest hearbs and roots. The third in place is the Goats dung, being most sower, that insueth the sheeps dung yet fatter. After this, both the Oxe and Cow dung, next the swines dung, worthier than the Oxen or Kine, but greatly disallowed of Columella, for the mighty hotnesse in that the same burneth the seeds immediately bestowed in the earth. The vilest and worst of all dungs, after the opinion of the Greek writers of Husbandry, is the Horses and Mules, if either of these be bestowed alone in the earth; yet with the sower dungs mixed, either will profitably be abated or qualified. But the same especially is to be learned and observed of every Gardener and Husbandman, that they fatten not the earth, if it be possible, with dung of one yeare for the same, besides that is of no utility, it engendreth also many noisome wormes and kinds of vermine. . . . The dung which men make (if the same be not mixed with the rubbish, or dust swept out of the house) is greatly misliked, for that by nature it is hotter, and burneth the seeds sown in that earth.

In the nineteenth and twentieth centuries pigeon lofts for carrier and racing pigeons became a profitable hobby in industrial and urban areas, as delightfully portrayed in a vignette in the film *Little Voice*. The allotment movement grew up at the same time and the contents of pigeon lofts were diverted into another urban hobby, that of growing prize leeks and marrows.

Caged

Francis Bacon concluded his 1625 essay 'On Gardens' with the words:

> For aviaries, I like them not, except they be of that largeness as they may be turfed, and have living plants and bushes set in them; that the birds may have more scope, and natural nestling; and that no foulness appear in the floor of the aviary. So I have made a platform of a princely garden, partly by precept, partly by drawing not a model, but some general lines of it; and in this I have spared for no cost. But it is

nothing for great princes, that for the most part taking advice with workmen, with no less cost set their things together; and sometimes add statues, and such things, for state and magnificence, but nothing to the true pleasure of a garden.

The frontispiece to James Shirley Hibberd's *Rustic Adornments for Homes of Taste* includes a portrait of one of his parrots. Born in the village of Stepney on the eastern outskirts of London in 1825, Hibberd later lived in Lordship Terrace, Stoke Newington, where he wrote for his urban neighbours in Hackney and Islington. Many pages of *Rustic Adornments* are devoted to building and stocking an aviary, but he only mentions the word 'dung' twice, although his many other books eulogise about a variety of manures and dungs. To begin with, and with no further instruction, he wrote, rather darkly: 'In all cases the excrements of the birds will indicate the state of their health, and whether the food ought to be changed or not.' Did his readers know what was normal? Hibberd confides that he and his wife were not blessed with children but had a large and noisy family of parrots, so the following idea is unsurprising:

A parrot-house might very well be combined with a vinery, where, under the shadow of purple grapes a large number of choice birds would find sufficient room to be happy. Our design for a structure of this kind is in the Moorish style and is well adapted for use as an open bird and vine-house during summer. . . . A collection of parrots and paroquets would have a splendid effect in such a building, and give it a truly oriental appearance.

Customers are directed to Mr Hawkins of 6 Bear Street, Leicester Square, 'an extensive importer of the original Zollverien cages and a most conscientious dealer in birds of all kinds'. Furthermore, 'no lady need fear to enter his establishment and pick and choose from his extensive stock, and that, unfortunately, cannot be said of many of the London bird shops; the majority of them are dens that reek with effluvia . . .'.

Fowl Play

The anonymous mid-seventeenth-century *Treatise on Domestic Pigeons*, contains a section devoted to 'Their Dung', which opens: 'Having thus shewn you something of the usefulness of this Bird, both in food and physick, I cannot omit saying something of its most excrementitious part.' Claiming that one load is worth ten of any other dung, like Tusser the author reckoned it 'extraordinary good soil for a hop-garden' and added that tanners used it for tanning the upper leathers. If his readers took the trouble to pick, sift and deliver it, they could earn 8*d* per bushel. He even included a recipe for saltpetre:

> a mixture of Pigeons dung, fowls dung, hogs dung, fat earth, and lime, which with another ingredient will form salt-petre, only it must be kept covered with a shed, to prevent or keep off the rain, that it may only mix with the nitrous quality of the air; . . . the saltpetre men produce it after this manner to this very day . . .

Quoting Dr Salmon for dung's medicinal uses, the following recipe is suggested for the treatment of baldness: 'Of the powder of the dung, bears grease, pepper in powder, oil of cummin-seed; mix them for an ointment'. Other recipes are given for 'scrophulous' and other hard tumours, while to ripen a plague sore, 'Of the dung in powder, black soap, oil of amber, mithridate; mix them for a cataplasm . . .'.

In Chapter 2, 'Architectural Movements', I described the pigeon towers of Isfahan. Interestingly, the anonymous treatise includes a 'story out of Tavernier, in the fourth book of his first volume of Persian travels', which describes the keeping of pigeons in those parts:

> As for their Pigeons, they fly wild about the country, but only some which they keep tame in the city, to decoy the rest, which is a sport the Persians use in hot weather as well as cold. Now in regard the Christians are not permitted to keep these Pigeons, some of the vulgar

sort will turn Mahometans to have that liberty. There are above three thousand Pigeon-houses in Ispahan, for every man may build a pigeon-house upon his own farm, which yet is very rarely done. All the other pigeon-houses belong to the king, who draws a greater revenue from the dung than from the Pigeons; which dung, as they prepare it, serves to smoak their melons.

Dung Fowl

There are more domestic hens, *Gallus domesticus*, on Earth than any other bird species. They are descendants of *Gallus gallus* and originated from the tropical regions of Asia. Their large sharp nails are excellent for foraging through the leaf litter on the forest floor for insects, worms and seeds, habits that are a joy to watch in any free-range hen. They live in flocks presided over by a dominant cockerel who is ornamental, aggressive and largely uneconomic. Traditional advice for finding the plumpest hen for the table was to go out at night and take the hen perching closest to the cock. Fully free-range hens offer a negligible amount of dunging but folded free range gives the soil a fertility boost and reduces the insect population. A traditional strawyard approximates to the hens' natural forest environment, and the litter can be dry leaves, wood shavings, peat moss, spoiled hay, grain husks or pea straw. Hard-working hens pick over the mixture and convert it into a rich compost. Mobile arks are superb as well and the pure dung from henhouses can be put straight on the compost heap as an activator.

Our family kept free-range hens for years, and Hilda especially enjoyed joining the family on a rug in the sun. My first reference book was *The Backyard Poultry Book* by Andrew Singer, which describes a novel method of using hens to improve your soil, invented by one Bernard Capon. He put a small amount of whole grain into the diet of his cattle, and when the cows were moved on the hens were put into their field at the rate of six to the acre. The hens diligently scratched away at the dry cowpats to extract any undigested grain, ate all the nematodes and spread the muck evenly at the same time.

Closely confined hens also produce poultry manure but without the joy. And now, such is the potency of the manure and so great the risk of it leaching into watercourses, in England there is actually a closed period for poultry manure. At the time of writing farmers must not spread poultry manure on grass or autumn-sown crops on sandy or shallow soils from 1 September to 1 November. This prohibition may soon be extended to all soils until 1 December.

Guano

A chain of small uninhabited islands off the coast of South America, notably the Chinchas, provides breeding sites for pelicans, albatrosses and other oceanic birds, with the more propitious sites appearing positively urban in the density of nests. The young birds demand and consume vast quantities of fish from their parents. Invariably messy feeders, they excrete copiously and some die, and to this potent mix can be added seaweed, stones and shells. Once the birds have fledged and flown, the abandoned mulched sites bake under the tropical sun and the intense dryness of the atmosphere prevents the accumulated materials from fermenting. Long before the arrival of Spanish adventurers in the region, local populations had been harvesting the potent fertiliser as a way to ensure good crops. In 1804 Alexander Von Humboldt, impressed by the trade that the Peruvians had created, brought samples back to Europe from the Chinchas Islands. However, it was not until early in 1840 that the first shipments were landed in Liverpool and by 1845 some 283,300 tons were reaching the United Kingdom.

Farmers in both Europe and the United States needed better yields from their crops. In North America the demand was initially met by guano deposits in North Carolina and other southern states, until scientists analysed the efficacy of guano from different reserves. The results showed that the best (nitrate-rich) types were found in excessively dry climates, as rainwater leached away the nitrates. British and European interests were already well established in Peru, and the British negotiated a monopoly on the mining and export of guano from the region. This pushed up the price for American buyers to unacceptable levels, so the search began for alternative stocks.

The prodigious gardening writer Jane Loudon, who urged ladies to don their gloves and garden, wrote in 1846: 'Guano. A new kind of manure, lately introduced from South America. It consists of the dung of sea fowls . . . it is so strong that a table-spoonful of it dissolved in water will go as far as three trowels-full of horse-dung. It may be used for Orange-trees, Pelargoniums, Heart's-Ease, Fuchsias, and any other plants requiring rich soil.'

Today, as farmers and gardeners move increasingly towards organic methods, interest has revived in guano. One company, Guano Australia Pty Ltd, is taking the lead in promoting organic and sustainable farming industries for the twenty-first century.

A Good Bat

Bat guano is closely allied to seabird guano but only small quantities were collected from caves in America and South Africa during the nineteenth century and never reached commercial proportions. However, it is now being marketed as the best organic fertiliser in the world. Universal and odourless, it is ideal for fruit, vegetables, bushes and trees. It is available via the internet; type in www.bat-guano.com for prices and availability. Bats in the roof or the belfry are a nightmare of misplaced dung, but wild bat caves are another of nature's marvels.

In 2004 Nicola Davies, writing about the Bracken Cave colony of 20 million bats in Texas, described 50 tons of droppings falling daily to the ground. Back in the 1900 'new' edition of *Thompson's Gardener's Assistant* the section on manure included the following:

Bat's or Texas Guano – This manure is imported from Texas, where it accumulates in considerable quantities in caves frequented by large

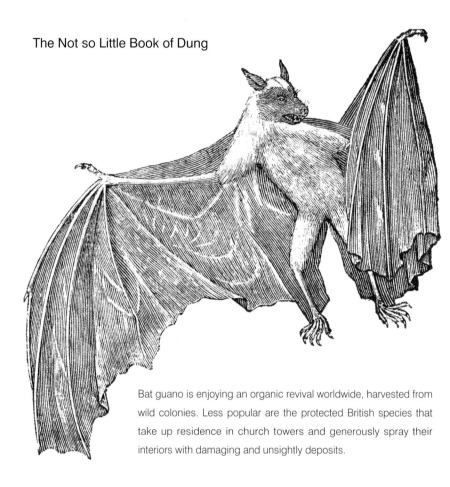

Bat guano is enjoying an organic revival worldwide, harvested from wild colonies. Less popular are the protected British species that take up residence in church towers and generously spray their interiors with damaging and unsightly deposits.

numbers of bats, of which it is the dried excrement. A microscopic examination shows the remains of their insect diet. According to Dr Voelcker's analysis, bats' guano contains nitrogen in three separate forms – as organic matter, as ammonia salts, and in the form of nitrates. Hence the nitrogen is in different degrees of solubility. The nitrates are ready for immediate absorption by the roots of plants. The ammonia salts may first of all undergo a change with the ultimate formation of nitrates; and, lastly, the organic matter requires time for its decomposition; therefore it forms a reserve or latent supply of nitrogen, which becomes active after a time.

Recent researchers studying the guano of a colony of 150 insect-eating big brown bats in Arizona discovered that they consumed 18 million insect pests in just one summer. The bat caves at Blanchards Springs Cavern in Arkansas has become a tourist attraction. There are three levels of cave, the lowest of which is left to the bats so that they continue 'untouched by human hand'. Visitors can take a themed tour of the upper two levels and glimpse the huge hill of ancient bat guano displayed on the first floor.

Davies also described researchers skiing over the hills of guano, which are alive not with music but with coprophages such as pinhead-sized mites and 3cm-long cockroaches. In turn these make tasty snacks for toads, which become dinner for snakes and opossums – a divine circle of content. Niah Cave in Burma is the only place on Earth to boast a coprophage earwig and an earwig-eating gecko. Bats are also useful in other ways. Fruit bats, for example, are invaluable spreaders of shrubs, trees and tropical fruits, swooping down at night to devour the fruits that hang clear of the bushes and then processing them en route back to their roosts.

The Rousette or Great Ternate Bat illustrated in this chapter is taken from *A General History of Quadrapeds* (1792). After a physical description, Thomas Bewick wrote about its habits:

Water (loss at 212°), ...		20·10
(1) Organic matter and combined water, ...		50·13
(2) Phosphoric acid, ...		6·37
Lime, ...		12·19
Iron oxide, alumina and alkali salt, ...		8·58
Insoluble silica, ...		2·63
		100·00
(1) Total nitrogen (including 2·56 nitric nitrogen),		8·45
Equal to ammonia, ...		10·26
(2) Tribasic phosphate, ...		13·90

The microscopic examination of bat guano 'imported from Texas' shows the remains of the bats' insect diet. According to Dr Voelcker's analysis, bat guano contains nitrogen in three separate forms, organic matter, ammonia salts and nitrates.

They feed on fruits, and are extremely fond of the juice of the palm-tree, with which they will frequently intoxicate themselves, so as to drop on the ground. One hundred and fifty or two hundred of them may sometimes be seen on the same tree, all hanging with their heads down, and their wings folded; and in this manner they repose during a great part of the day. – They grow very fat at certain times of the year; and when young, they are eaten by the Indians, and considered as excellent food.

Bewick also included a description of the 'Spectre Bat . . . called the Vampyre by M. Buffon; who supposes it to be one of the blood-sucking tribe. Its nose is long and at the end there is a membrane, of a conical form, somewhat like a horn, but flexile, which gives it a hideous and disgusting aspect. It has no tail. Its body is covered with long hair, of an ash colour.' Diet dictates the content of guano, and that of the vampire bat is the messiest because of its diet of blood (rarely human); its droppings resemble runny jam. For the record the bumblebee bat (not mentioned by Bewick), which weighs just 3g, produces some of the smallest droppings, the size of a pinhead.

Such was the selling power of guano that the word was attached to other potential fertilisers such as meat guano and greaves. Meat guano was prepared from slaughterhouse refuse including carcasses, condemned meat, bones, tallow boilers' refuse and residues from meat extracts. These were heated, pressed to remove the fat and finely ground. In America this process was called tankage. By the early twentieth century Fray Bentos, who had cornered the market in corned beef, started to manufacture the fine friable Fray Bentos Guano. Writing in 1909 A.D. Hall reported that this meat guano contained 7 per cent nitrogen and 3 per cent phosphate of lime, and instructed that it should be ploughed in immediately to prevent birds (especially rooks) feasting on it. In the wake of BSE and the salmonella scare it is interesting to note that an alternative use for meat guano – and commanding a higher price – was as a cattle or poultry feed. For the benefit of crossword fans and players of word games, the term for low-grade meat guano (made from the waste from tallow making, scraps of cartilage and bone) is greaves.

Fowl Fancy

Humans suffering from fox predation in their gardens are advised to get the men of the house to mark out their territory with urine. A male fox will not risk trespassing on the territory of a larger, more powerful male. A similar device was adapted by African waxbills, who deter possible predators by scenting their nests with carnivore dung collected from the savannah. Lion dung from the Longleat Estate in Wiltshire has been used to build walls to deter deer and rabbits; this is very effective, but unfortunately only while the air is redolent with the fresh odour.

Edward Lear's Pussycat described his owl companion as an elegant fowl as they sailed away in their pea-green boat. Wise and elegant as most owls certainly are, the burrowing owl, *Athene cunicularia*, is a bird of unusual habits. Recently these birds have been the subject of research by the University of Florida. The owl's habitat is open prairie and semi-desert regions from Canada to Chile, and also Florida. A small diurnal owl with long legs, it usually nests in prairie dog 'towns' and, oddly, can be found around airports in Florida. They perch on the ground or a post, bobbing up and down with a quick bending movement of their legs outside the deep holes in the ground where they nest: but are they guarding the entrance to their treasured collections or is there a bigger prize?

At their burrow entrance the owls create a display that typically includes bits of glittering foil and pieces of plastic, partly chewed centipede and squashed toads carefully scraped off the road, as well as shreds of cowpat, diced horse droppings and dollops of bison dung. (In the past one can only assume they contented themselves with centipedes and bison dung.) The dung is highly prized and they will fly several hundred metres to collect it; if any is removed from the burrow forecourt, it is replaced within four days. Intrigued by this dung devotion, a group of scientists from the University of Florida in Gainesville have undertaken research observation. Were the burrowing owls using similar tactics to those of the African waxbills to camouflage their nests? Apparently not. However, among the regurgitated pellets containing beaks and bones there was a preponderance of the hard outer parts of beetles including several species of dung beetle. Trials were set up using the entrances to ten burrows, which were cleaned of all traces of dung and beetle. Five were left bare and the other five provided with cow dung. Initially the researchers enthusiastically introduced moist dung – a gourmet treat for many dung beetles but not the Australian variety – before realising that it would just ooze out between the owls' talons, so they settled for dung dry enough for an owl to transport but moist enough to attract dung beetles.

After four days they collected all the pellets and prey remains from the ten burrows, and then the experiment was reversed and repeated. The trial showed conclusively that the owls with the dung ate ten times the quantity of dung beetles. Presumably then, the owls sit on the posts and wait for their prey to come to them!

7

LIQUID ASSETS

Trampling th'unshowered grass with lowings loud.

John Milton, Paradise Lost *(1667)*

Natural Reserves

Water, running, still or precipitate, transforms raw dung into a ready-mixed rich silt. The Valley of Mexico (which at 7,000ft above sea level is hardly what one thinks of as a valley) is encircled by high mountain chains whose wooded slopes shelter an abundance of deer and other creatures. During the rainy season alluvial deposits enriched with wildlife dung is washed down into the valley. Agriculture in the region has been dated back to 1,500 BC around the great salt lake of Texcoco, which is fed at its southerly shores by two sweet water lagoons, Xochimilco and Chalco, from the north-west by Xaltocan and Zumpango, and by the sluggish Acolman river draining out of the Valley of Teotihuacan in the north-east. The shores of these shallow lakes are marshy and teeming with wildfowl. Human communities sprang up at the most convenient sites for farming corn, cotton, beans and other vegetables, as well as harvesting the natural resources of the forest and lakes.

The penning and domestication of animals did not enter into this agricultural cycle. Bison and caribou roamed wild, but cow and sheep were unknown. Nor did the people have horses for transport so they tended to stay put. A non-watery by-product of this has proved to be an archaeologist's dream, as their refuse simply accumulated into middens up to 25ft deep. These vast compost heaps of human excrement, animal bones, broken pottery and bulky vegetable matter like corn shocks decayed into soft, churned earth, which sometimes also served as burial sites. Presumably the people were not bothered by large fly colonies and a ripe stench.

Present-day Mexico City was colonised by the Aztecs in the fourteenth century. Arriving as slaves and migrants, they initially survived on floating islands in Lake Tenochitlán. To avoid hunger, they diligently scraped up the silt from the lake bottom and deposited it on their small plots so that they could grow sub-sistence vegetables. When the Spanish Conquistadores arrived two centuries later they were mightily impressed, and Bernal Diaz, the soldier and historian, described walking through fine stands of trees, waterfalls and basins as well as cages of rare birds and people with unusual defects. Three magnificent causeways approached the city from the north, west and south, each flanked by canals. Further water for the city was provided by two aque-ducts, one of which (from Chapultepec) was constructed with two channels to ensure a constant supply of fresh water if one was broken or under repair. The streets of Tenochitlán were little more than canals, bordered by footpaths and frequently crossed by bridges for ease of access. Boats tied up at regular intervals were used as public conveniences, and when full their contents were bartered as fertiliser for the fields. At home people used pottery vessels for urine, which was then sold as a mordant for dyeing cloth.

In the words of Diaz:

> Then Montezuma took Cortés by the hand and told him to look at his great city and all the other cities that were standing in the water and the many other towns and land around the lake . . . and we saw three causeways which led into Mexico . . . and we saw the fresh water that comes from Chapultepec, which supplies the city . . . and it was a wonderful thing to behold!

Sadly, in 1521 the Spaniards sacked the floating city and effectively pulled out the plug – and all these wonders disappeared without trace. But the Spanish paid a heavy price for their destructiveness, for in the process they lifted the lid on the pestilence that then beset them.

According to the ancient oracle of the god Amun, 'Egypt is the land watered by the Nile in its course; and those who dwell below the city Elephantine and drink that river's water are Egyptians.' Once a year the waters of the Nile, teeming with life, flooded its vast valley, leaving behind a generously thick deposit. This process dictated Egypt's three seasons – of brown, green and gold. The enriching brown season began when the floodwaters receded, having renewed the fertility of the flood plain, but the building of the Aswan dam brought this cycle to an abrupt end. Once the soil was dry enough to work, the farmers would round up their serfs, their long-horned African cows and their goats ready for the next process. Armed with baskets of grain (either barley or wheat), the serfs walked along in front of the cows, drawing ploughs with shallow wooden shares, followed by the goats. The wooden plough shares turn in the seed while the heavy hooves of the cows and the goats' pattering feet ensured the seed was firmly set, and any added extras from the animals were regarded as a bonus. This was followed by the 'green' season as all the newly planted crops germinated and sprouted, and this in turn, disasters permitting, was followed by the 'gold' or harvest season. This cycle was indirectly captured in Sam Johnson's neat definition of 'unshowered' as 'not watered by showers', illustrated with an apt quotation from Milton:

> Nor is Osiris seen
> In Memphian grove or green,
> Trampling th'unshowered grass with lowings loud.

The floating gardens of Amiens in France, the *Hortillonages*, were first cultivated by the Romans to provide food for their troops. For two thousand years the black soil has been fed with dungy silt and mineral deposits brought by the regular flooding of these fertile marshes. From the medieval period onward the area was the market garden for Paris. Today some 300 hectares have survived, along with the traditional wooden buildings, despite the lack of a modern transport system (they use a network of canals) and electricity. Its fertility has ensured its survival. Organic produce is sold at local markets and once a year the *maraichers* hold a river market.

Ancient Roman gardens such as that at Hadrian's Villa at Tivoli near Rome celebrated the Nile delta in its magnificent outdoor dining-room, the Canopus. Here, a peristyled limpid pool was dominated by the elaborate triclinium, with an army of slaves to keep it clean and bright. What a contrast to the awfulness of the River Tiber, engorged with the contents of the Cloaca Maxima, especially at the height of summer. Over a thousand years later the River Thames was not much better as it swelled with London's swill. There was even a public latrine that discharged directly into the water from London Bridge.

Riparian Rewards

The Fenlands skirt The Wash in the eastern counties of Lincolnshire, Cambridgeshire and Norfolk, and the soil here is considered the finest agricultural tilth in England. Its fertile depths originated from a flooded plain lapped by Jurassic clays and banded by the chalklands of present-day Norfolk and Suffolk to the south and east and (to a lesser extent) Lincolnshire to the north; to the west are the limestones and sandstones of Cambridgeshire's Middle Jurassic Scarp Belt. Rising out of this plain are several 'islands', such as Ely and March, historically reached by boat and causeway but now little more than architectural pinnacles in the flat farmland.

The assorted waste found in post-glacial deposits laid down silts and clays on the seaward sides, inevitably with a tendency to salinity, but the agricultural 'gold' lay on the landward side in the form of deep rich peat. Around the time of the Roman occupation the sea level had dropped, as a result of which the ancient rivers, now known as 'roddons', had silted up, creating higher land for dry travel, building and crops. From the medieval era onwards the soil was hard-won from rising tidal incursions and sluggish streams and rivers. Writing in the thirteenth century Matthew Paris noted:

> Concerning this marsh a wonder has happened in our time; for in the years past, beyond living memory, these places were accessible neither for man nor for beast, affording only deep mud with sedge and reeds, and inhabited by birds, indeed more likely by devils as appears from the life of St Guthlac who began to live there and found it a place of horror and solitude. This is now changed into delightful meadows and also arable ground. What therefore does not produce corn or hay brings forth abundance, sedge, turf and other fuel, very useful to the inhabitants of the region.

It was truly a pastoral idyll but the notion of horror, solitude and devils continue to colour the writings of many visitors to the damp, malarial Fens, despite the divine spectacle of the abbey of Ely rising out of the unhealthy mists.

The potential of this rich and seemingly fathomless black loam attracted Elizabethan entrepreneurs. Various reclamation schemes were discussed and negotiated, but there was little actual progress. Plans continued under both Charles I and Oliver Cromwell. The Duke of Bedford offered to put in the necessary channels or sewers and dykes in exchange for the extension of his land by 95,000 acres! Dutchman Cornelius Vermuyden, who had successfully drained and gained land in Holland and in 1621 mended the breach of the River Thames at Dagenham, was approached and agreed to reclaim and drain land in exchange for 90,000 acres. But the xenophobic Fenlanders were 'not liking to contract to an alien or a stranger', let alone the specialist Dutch workforce he might introduce. Nevertheless after much discussion and generous land allocation to key officials, work started in 1634, and by 1652 Vermuyden had successfully reclaimed some 301,000 acres (122,000 hectares) of the Bedford Level. Whereas guano requires a

Riparian meadows were often deliberately flooded with nutrient-enriched river water to provide richer pasture. The haystacks in the background evoke September in M. Stevenson's 1661 poem 'The Twelve Moneths': 'In a word the whispering woods are now fain to quit their leavie pretences and come to the naked truth; the Meadows are left bare by the mouths of the hungry Cattel, and the Hogs (those four-footed Swains) are become the Plowers of the Corn-fields.'

dry climate for maximum development, the anaerobic rotting process of sedges, rushes and other vegetation formed fabulously fertile peat, largely thanks to faecal pellets and much dung seepage.

While sheep and goats can graze the grasses and flowers of poor soils and survive in harsh conditions (resulting in such culinary delights as Welsh lamb served with wild thyme from the Welsh hillsides), beef and dairy cattle require the richer pasture found in river valleys. Thus many riparian meadows were routinely flooded in spring, the shallow running water helping to warm the soil and its nutrients boosting new grass growth. In 1793 W. Elstobb published *An Historical Account of the Great Level of the Fens, called Bedford Level and other Fens, Marshes and Lowlands in this Kingdom and other Places*, itemising who was prepared to do what and for how much land or money. The successful draining of the Fens, as with many of the Agrarian Revolution improvements, helped large-scale farmers, but yeoman farmers, often tradesmen such as builders whose families ran smallholdings to see them through hard times, could not make the necessary investment and therefore became impoverished. Elstobb reported that of the 5,700 acres of common fen around Lakenheath, some 1,400 were sheep pastures that benefited from occasional flooding by 'wind-catches'. He went on:

> Methwold and other towns bordering upon the . . . Level, described the condition of it in much the same manner: . . . sheep walks for 1,700 sheep, which fed winter and summer, upon their common fens; and that when any floods happened they came by wind-catches, and run over but some part of their grounds, and continued not long, so that they were not damaged, but made better by such overflowings; and on those grounds they keep three or four hundred milch cows for dairies, and fed their working horses, and bred store of young cattles.

In 1877 S.B.J. Skertchly published *The Geology of the Fenland*:

> The greatest thickness attained by the peat, so far as I have ascertained, is 18 feet, in the parish of Earith. A like thickness was pierced in the parish of Warboys. . . . In the arm which stretches up to Lincoln and forms the valley of the Witham the peat occasionally attains a thickness of from six to eight feet. . . . From Heckington to Deeping Fen the peat is thin, seldom attaining a greater thickness than three feet, and is more frequently less than a foot. . . . The average thickness of the peat in the Bedford Level may be taken at about six feet, but it is very variable.

Until comparatively recently crop production alongside rivers and watercourses saved a great deal of labour when watering. In addition, travel and delivery to and from farms, market gardens and homes was quickest by water. Hyll's *The Gardener's Labyrinth* included sensible advice for Tudor householders: 'the aptest and most laudable placing of a Garden plot shall be . . . that have a course of spring water running thorow by several parts. . . . some running water, as either ditch or small River be near adjoyning; for that a sweet water sprinkled on young plants and herbs, giveth a special nourishment'. This nourishment and warmth were in contrast to the chill barrenness of water drawn from a well, though the author suggests improving the latter by mixing in a reasonable quantity of dung and standing it in the sun to warm.

To ensure a good supply of natural water Hyll recommended digging a pit, stating that he agreed with Columella that September was the best month to do so, presumably to take advantage of the equinox and autumnal rains. He advised people living near a city to have a well-dunged garden adjacent to the house, and to avoid as far as possible 'the vapours of standing pits, ditches, and

What do you get if you lie down in a cow pasture? A pat on the back. Compare the male and female scenes – the bull chasing the fleeing figure and the gently ruminating cow complete with fresh cow pat.

such like mixed to it, [because it] doth . . . choke and dul the spirits of men'.

In the eighteenth century Stephen Switzer found another benefit for gardeners: 'River water, especially such as it is about London, or any great city, where it is continually disturb'd and made thick by its own motions, and the soil of the washings of the streets and grounds, is much better for watering than either spring or rain water.' Traditionally most large-scale watering was done with buckets directly to the soil, as eating leafy crops from this regime would not be conducive to either taste or good health.

In 1850 the *Journal* of the Royal Agricultural Society published a paper by Professor J.T. Way entitled 'Composition and Money Value of Guano', in which he compared the fertilising ingredients of sewage and guano. In reply J.J. Mechi of Tiptree Hall, Kelvedon in Essex, and a London Alderman described 'the gradual but sure exhaustion of the soil of Great Britain by our new sanitary arrangements, which permit the excrements (really the food) of 15 million people, who inhabit our towns and cities, to flow wastefully into our rivers. The continuance of this suicidal practice must ultimately result in great calamities to our nation.' The *City Press* on 19 November 1864 offered a solution: 'There can be no doubt that the Maplin sands can be made to smile with golden harvests by means of fertilising slush that has so long been devoted to the poisoning of the Thames.' Half a century later the quest for nitrogenous fertilisers was furthered by fish guano, created from the processing residues from canning and curing sardines and herrings. Just like the real thing, when dried and reduced to powder this slowly released nitrogen into the soil. As it was also injurious to germinating seeds and young plants it was the favoured fertiliser for Edwardian hop-growers.

Channelled Energy

The Alhambra tops the Sabika Hill above Granada in Spain, shaped like a boat moored on the fertile plains below the Sierra

Nevada. From the ninth century the water so essential in such arid conditions was ingeniously harnessed and channelled from the snowy peaks by the Moors. The Alhambra complex comprises the *Alcazaba*, *Palacios*, *Medina* and *Generalife*, but it is most famed for its '*patios*' in the *Palacios* and *Generalife* (or Summer Palace). The Moorish Nasrid dynasty (1237–1492) designed these palaces around *patios* whose inner (spiritual) beauty centred on brimming pools and narrow rills, in stunning contrast to the plain exteriors. The *Patio de los Leones*, surrounded by a 'forest' of marble pillars and intricate stucco, led the visitor to the twelve lions supporting a fountain basin topped with a further gently bubbling bowl (the latter now up on the ramparts). The fountains in turn fed the network of rills, beautifully expressed in the engraved script:

Water and marble seem as one, so we know not which of the two flows. Do you not see how the water spills over the basin, but is hidden forthwith in the channels? It is a lover whose eyelids brim with tears; tears which then hide in fear of betrayal. Is it not, in reality but a

Multi-purpose water from the Sierra Nevada: it was ornamental on the patio, cleansing in the latrines and finally nutritive on the vegetable terraces between the Alhambra and *Generalife* in Granada.

white mist emptying its waters on the lions and resembling the hand of the caliph, which in the morning, lavishes favours on the lions of war?

Beautiful and functional, the rills continue on their journey, and having fulfilled a spiritual need they then perform the more mundane task of answering bodily needs in the kitchens and latrines, well away from prying eyes. The slopes of the hillsides between the public and private palace of the *Generalife* were (and still are) ridged for vegetables irrigated by these enriched waters.

Today's visitors climbing the steps to the tower beyond the *Generalife* can cool their hands in the swirling waters while contemplating the words of Juan Ramon Jimenez: 'I heard that music of the water more and more yet at the same time less; less because it was no longer an intimate of mine; the water was my blood, my life and I heard that the music of my life and blood was the running water.'

Status Symbol

The garderobes in medieval castles and Tudor manor-houses were designed mostly to decant directly into their moats. The tower-houses of northern England and Scotland were less frequently moated, so their garderobes discharged into projecting turrets or bartizans, below which barrels were lined up. Once full, these were removed and the contents put to good use.

Moats could be rectangular, round or square, with single or double platforms on which a building might or might not be constructed. How upmarket to be rowed across to a moated private garden adorned with arbours and scented plants away from the common herd. Some moats were dry but water-filled moats around castles, manor-houses and farmsteads provided richer pickings. Moat construction was largely undertaken between 1150 and 1500, peaking between 1200 and 1325, incidentally a period of hot, sunny summers. Moats were traditionally created

A village pond being excavated in 2005 to remove accumulated duck droppings which were not allowed to be put on the fields.

for defensive purposes, but their ornamental value as mirrors around grand houses ensured their continued creation.

Today we turn up our noses all too quickly at seemingly unhygienic practices, forgetting the historic seasoned balancing of everyday life. Manorial households would move between several properties, living off the land and stores, while moats were populated by pike and carp which consumed the refuse, added elegant ornamentation and provided food for the table. Well managed as a constantly renewable resource, at intervals the moat was emptied and redug and the spoil spread on the land, ensuring minimal stink. The Revd Samuel Gilbert in *The Florist's Vade Mecum* (1683) compared the efficacious properties of 'green slime of still water' with horse, deer and asses' dung in the bid to produce fine flowers. Those whose house was moated or perhaps contained a small pool

The glorious gardens of Coton Manor are enhanced by the pool and the gurgling stream, with their resident population of ducks, hens, flamingoes and a parrot.

might be troubled by noisy frogs. What they needed was the Lamp of Alberto, created from a recipe in an Italian manual of fortune-telling and necromancy. The lamp was created from a mixture of sun-blanched wax and crocodile fat, with a wick incorporated as it cooled. Lit and left on the bank, it would silence the frogs.

8

EXOTIC RESOURCES

The Bonasus . . . a wild beast of Paeonia . . . with a mane like an horse, otherwise resembling a bull: . . . This ordure of his is so strong and hot, that it burneth them that follow after him in chase . . .

Pliny the Elder, Naturalis Historia *(AD 1)*

Purity of Purpose

Pliny describes the wild beast of Paeonia who, when angered, squirted his red hot dung over 3 acres at a time (giving a whole new meaning to the phrase 'scorched earth policy'). Could Pliny have been referring to the male hippopotamus, who by waggling his tail sprays his macho dung-laden message over considerable distances? Pliny also chronicled multiple uses of dung, such as cat

The male hippopotamus waggles his bristly 1ft-long tail as he defecates in order to spread the message of his virility as widely as possible. Hippos leave the safety of the water at night to graze on the grass around the lake; to ensure their safe return they leave a faecal trail as a navigational aid.

Peccaries create large communal latrines. They hunt and forage alone, so their dung acts like a noticeboard to their fellows, relaying vital information about gender, age, inclination and travel arrangements.

dung attached to the arm as a preventative for ague, neat's (sheep) dung for dropsy and boar's dung gathered in spring for convulsions, cramps and nerve strain. Today diligent dog owners arm themselves with bags when they go for walkies, depriving dogs of their sniff-and-tell habits and thankfully us from the traditional good luck engendered by stepping in it. Such walkers are a less profitable echo of the 'pure finders' who collected and sold dog excrement to tanners. Nineteenth-century leatherworkers and skinners rubbed it into the animal skins to purify them.

Identifying droppings is an ancient skill perfected by hunters in every species, and now mastered by anthropologists, zoologists, archaeologists and sometimes dieticians. Anyone who has had problems with mice knows that they leave a trail of tiny black trademarks absolutely everywhere. The mysteries of the deep are revealed by sperm whales whose hunting grounds lie some 8,000ft below the surface. Prior to their great dives they evacuate their bowels, so oceanographers nifty with a net can catch a digested stew of known and unknown submarine life including squid up to 65ft long.

In 2004 Tring Museum hosted a splendid exhibition entitled 'Poo – A Natural History of the Unmentionable'. Inspired by Nicola Davies's book, it was not just illustrated by model animals, droppings and drawings but was also a lift-the-lid-and-smell experience! For an animal, a good sniff can tell them all they need to know: who produced it and when, and their age, sex and sexual availability. Peccaries, a form of wild pig inhabiting the South

American jungle, live in groups and create a latrine at the heart of their territory so that on their return from seeking food they can catch up on the news with just a sniff or two. Other animals use dung in different ways. The caterpillar of the Australian citrus swallowtail butterfly, for example, has perfected the art of disguise, and looks for all the world like a bird dropping.

Menagerie Manure

Exotic muck – and money – is being made in the Surrey Hills. Che Guevara is one of eight llamas at the heart of a new dung operation. Llamas have offensive urine but odourless dung, which emerges ready pelleted. What traditionally would be described as short dung is marketed as 'Che Guevara's Number Two', with the advantage that it can be spread fearlessly around plants. In contrast the manurial benefits of dung from tigers and lions are enhanced by their reputation for deterring deer and cats. As carnivores they produce long untidy dung containing hair, fur, feathers, bone and any undigested parts of their prey. It has an unmistakable smell, and dung walls made of it will keep at bay potential prey (but only until the smell fades). The lions at Longleat in Wiltshire were among the first to have their dung marketed.

Attention to the diets of dung providers are key to the end product. The fruit and vegetable diet of some of the residents of Paignton Zoo, such as the black rhinos Kingo and Sita and the elephants Gay and Duchess, results in solid waste packed with nutrients and trace elements. Keen to share their rich droppings and help the animals earn their keep, we can now buy Zoo Poo 'Jumbo enriched' in 10-litre bags. It is also possible to unzip a banana courtesy of Woburn Safari Park, which supports an Asian elephant conservation scheme with the home elephantine efforts of Damini, Shandrika and Raja. Jointly they produce one of the key ingredients in the 'Poo Planter' box, the other is seeds of the pink banana, *Musa velutina*, delivered direct to your door. But working the soil to create comestible delicacies is not confined to the human world. There are species of termite which allow wood to pass through their systems without digesting it. The ensuing product is formed into lumps called combs. These are placed deep within the termite hill, their soft texture providing ideal growing conditions for mushrooms – convenience food for the termite colony!

A healthy diet in the wild entails building up your digestive strength, and baby elephants will eat their mother's dung – just once – to inherit her immunities. In Australia Koala bears eat tough eucalyptus leaves which are extremely indigestible and full of poisons. But nature has provided the Koala with special microbes that live in their gut and aid the digestive process, and these microbes have to be passed from mother to child. The cub is weaned on portions of its mother's droppings so that the microbes can settle in and get to work.

Antediluvian Deposits

Faecal pellets are probably present in most geological sediments but they are rarely recognised because of their dispersion among other material. The pellets are formed from small masses of the ovoid and occasionally rod-shaped excreta of invertebrates such as molluscs and echinoderms. Deposits of fossilised faecal pellets of fish, reptiles, birds and mammals are known as coprolites and are richly phosphatic in character. Good deposits were found by Professor Henslow at the base of the greensand near Cambridge, at other places in Suffolk and at Potton in Bedfordshire. They were first believed to be fossilised dinosaur dung, but this was wrongly dismissed and instead they were laboriously identified as pebbles of carbonate of lime in which the carbonic acid had been replaced by phosphoric acid by long contact with material containing organic matter. The need for fertilisers during the Second World War led to new mining and re-identification of the pellets as fossilised faecal matter – or in layman's terms, dinosaur droppings. In Canada coprolites were found alongside the bones of a Tyrannosaurus rex; the droppings contained fragments of a triceratop's rib bones scarred with the toothmarks of T. rex.

Dedicated Dung Eaters

There are 7,000 different types of dung beetle in the world, each neatly adapted to the task in hand. There are, for example, steeple-jacks which operate in the rainforest canopy cleaning leaves of monkey excreta and neatly burying it in the forest floor, and small species that tidy up ready-rounded rabbit pellets. Desert dung beetles cope with the rock-hard droppings of water-conserving camels by burying it in moist sand until it becomes malleable, while Australian dung beetles are adept with kangaroo and wallaby pellets.

Jean Henri Fabre (1823–1915), the great French devotee and observer of the dung beetle, was born in St Léons, Aveyron, and eventually retired to live in Sérignon. His longing to travel the world and explore was diverted into the closest observation of the insect life that surrounded him; he was fascinated by tiny insect villages, fruit branches hosting praying mantis, bushes where pale Italian crickets would strum, dung-clad blades of grass scraped by the *Anthidium*, clusters of lilac worked by the leaf-cutter *Megachile*. His neighbours were ever vigilant on Fabre's behalf. One of them, a young shepherd, found for him a

> pear . . . prettier in shape than agate marble, much more graceful than an ivory egg or a box-wood top. The material, it is true, seems none too nicely chosen; but it is firm to the touch and very artistically

curved. . . . My excitement could have been no greater were I an archaeologist digging among the ancient relics of Egypt and lighting upon the sacred insect of the dead, carved in emerald, in some Pharaonic crypt. O blessed joys of truth suddenly shining forth, what others are there to compare with you!

That morning Fabre found a further dozen pears made from 'stercoral' bread. He notes that the sacred beetle is also a fine baker, selecting from the dung of mules, horses, sheep and cattle. The first three are coarse and eaten by the mother but for her family:

> She now wants fine pastry, rich in nourishment and easily digested; she wants the ovine manna: not that which the sheep of a dry habit scatters in trails of black olives, but that which, elaborated in a less parched intestine, is kneaded into biscuits all of a piece. That is the material required, the dough exclusively used. It is no longer the poor and stringy produce of the horse, but an unctuous, plastic, homogeneous thing soaked through and through with nourishing juices. Its plasticity, its delicacy are admirably adapted to the artistic work of the pear, while its alimentary qualities suit the weak stomach of the new-born progeny. Little though the bulk be, the grub will here find sufficient food.

The dung ball the beetle creates and fashions into a pear shape contains her egg, which will develop into a grub requiring nourishment. She hollows out a recess in the tapering neck, with polished shiny walls – 'the tabernacle of the germ, the hatching-chamber' – while beneath the grub lies the lovingly prepared stercoral feast. The rind, egg and nutritive mass is in effect like a bird's egg, with a hard outer shell that prevents desiccation of the rich yolk.

All this was deeply fascinating but Fabre furthered his researches to investigate dung beetles all over the planet. He was in corres-pondence with Brother Judulian of the Lasalle College in Buenos Aires, who was dispatched to study the life and loves of the dung

Fabre's illustration conveys the hard work required to form the perfect sphere of dung and transport it.

beetles of the pampas. Fabre compared Judulian's reports with visiting Argentina on a magic carpet to see *Phanaeus Milo*, 'a square-chinned, short-legged Dung-worker which excels in the art of manufacturing gourds'. Back in Provence, Fabre described *Minotaurus typhoeus* as 'a fair-sized coleopteron, closely related to the Earth-borers, the Geotrupes. He is a peaceable, inoffensive creature, but even better-horned than Minos's bull.' *Minotaurus* favoured the sandy grazing grounds of sheep, tidying up their trails of black pellets. Serious scientist though he undoubtedly was, Fabre analysed the love life of the *Minotaurus* with Gallic passion:

> Do the husband and wife recognise each other among their fellows? Are they mutually faithful? . . . Sometimes, two burrows are side by side. Cannot the collector of provisions, on returning home, easily mistake the door and enter another's house? On his walks abroad, does he never happen to meet ladies taking the air who have not yet settled down; and is he then not forgetful of his first mate and ready for divorce?

Fabre experimented with a mix and match set of male and female *Minotaurus*, who obligingly paired in every variation – was this due to the unusual circumstances or was it the norm? He could not be sure, but he carefully observed how they burrowed down to lodge each egg in the sandy soil at the base of the burrow, and left us an extraordinary description of the process:

The mother, more skilled in nursery matters, occupies the lower floor. She alone digs, versed as she is in the properties of the perpendicular, which economises work while giving the greatest depth. She is the engineer, always in touch with the working-face of the gallery. The other is her journeyman-mason. He is stationed at the back, ready to load the rubbish on his horny hod. Later, the excavatrix becomes a baker: she kneads the cakes for the children into cylinders; the father is then her baker's boy. He fetches her from outside the wherewithal for making flour. As in every well-regulated household, the mother is minister of the interior, the father minister of the exterior. This would explain their invariable position in the tubular home. The future will tell us if these conjectures represent the reality as it is.

The miller holds himself in place using his four hind legs while the baker works tirelessly, reforming the softer material into the core and the stringy pieces into the crust.

For the moment, let us make ourselves at home and examine at leisure the central clod so laboriously acquired. It contains preserved foodstuffs in the shape of a sausage nearly as long and thick as one's finger. This is composed of a dark, compact matter, arranged in layers, which we recognise as the sheep-pellets reduced to morsels. Sometimes, the dough is fine and almost homogeneous from one end of the cylinder to the other; more often, the piece is a sort of hardbake, in which large fragments are held together by a cement of amalgam. The baker apparently varies the more or less finished confection of her pastry according to the time at her disposal.

Next, Fabre noted, the male took on the role of 'miller', breaking up the pellets into smaller pieces for the 'baker' at work at the base, ensuring a well-stocked nest for the emerging grub. Then comes the tragic end:

Lastly, worn out by his efforts, he leaves the house and goes to die outside, at a distance, in the open air. He has gallantly performed his duty as paterfamilias; . . . The mother, on her side, allows nothing to divert her from her housekeeping . . . kneading her cylindrical loaves, filling them with an egg, watching them until the exodus arrives. When the day comes for the autumnal merry-makings, she at last returns to the surface, accompanied by the young people, who disperse at will to feast in the regions frequented by the sheep. Thereupon, having nothing left to do, the devoted mother perishes.

Purple Prose

The ever-spreading railways in the Victorian era opened the way for many excellent business opportunities. Commercial violet production was one such. Among the most successful were Fred and William Westcott from Cofton in Devon, whose violets thrived not on fertiliser but on their own growth-enhancing formula of tailors' clippings mixed with dung and old woollen rags. Was this dung from the donkey whose cart carried the Westcotts' violets (in reused corset boxes) to Dawlish station each morning? The West-cotts specialised in the violet variety 'Princess of Wales', and were reputedly the first to have grown parma violets commercially.

Any residue of the scent of dung had to be separated from the sweet violets, symbols of faithfulness, humility and simplicity (and erotic love in medieval flower language). Indeed, nothing could be more appropriate for a gentleman to present to a lady. Always an eager recipient of flattery, Queen Victoria loved violets, and George Lee sent her a bunch of specially cultivated violets named 'Victoria regina'.

Stool for Scandal

Scatology and coprophilia remain at the margins of acceptance, plunging either into obscenity and pornography or diverting into surreal alternative art – in the form of cans of excrement and films such as *Salo*. *Jerry Springer: The Opera* is regarded as crude and blasphemous, with Jesus Christ depicted as a coprophiliac. Similarly the satirical cartoon *Popetown* has an opening scene where the Pope has smeared himself in shit with flies buzzing around him. Were the writers aware that in Malachi those who do not worship the Lord will be cursed: 'Behold I will corrupt your seed, and spread dung upon your faces, even the dung of your solemn feasts; and one shall take you away with it.'

Dung makes numerous appearances in the Bible, its translation varying from excreta to simple manurial matter such as bones and waste. (Interestingly, 'dust to dust' could equally be translated 'dung to dung'.) Dung is used figuratively to feed the soil and the soul. The use of dung to stoke the fire is a common practice in arid lands where wood is scarce but human excrement is rarely put to this purpose. So shocking food and fuel are juxtaposed in Chapter 4 of Ezekiel, which contains the following instructions:

> Take thou also unto thee wheat, and barley, and beans, and lentiles, and millet, and fitches, and put them in one vessel, and make thee

bread thereof, according to the number of the days that thou shalt lie upon thy side, three hundred and ninety days shalt thou eat thereof. And thy meat which thou shalt eat shall be by weight, twenty shekels a day: from time to time shalt thou eat it. Thou shalt drink also water by measure, the sixth part of an hin: from time to time shalt thou drink. And thou shalt eat it as barley cakes, and thou shalt bake it with dung that cometh out of man, in their sight. And the Lord said Even thus shall the children of Israel eat their defiled bread among the Gentiles, whither I will drive them. Then said I, Ah Lord God! behold my soul hath not been polluted: for from my youth up even till now have I not eaten of that which dieth of itself, or is torn in pieces; neither came there abominable flesh into my mouth. Then he said unto me, Lo I have given thee cow's dung for man's dung, and thou shalt prepare thy bread therewith. Moreover he said unto me, Son of man, behold, I will break the staff of bread in Jerusalem: and they shall eat bread by weight, and with care, and they shall drink water by measure, and with astonishment: That they may want bread and water, and be astonished one with another, and consume away for their iniquity.

Poor Ezekiel, he really did have a rough time, although God did relent and agree to the substitution of cow dung for human waste as fuel. As in most human traditions, Jewish dietary regulations would have forbidden human excrement to be used at all, as it would pollute the food. Traditional ovens were filled with the faggots of wood which were lit, and once the oven was heated the dough was placed in the ashes. So if dung was used as fuel the bread would come into direct contact with the cremated dung – human or cow, it is an exceedingly unsavoury prospect. This can be interpreted as God's punishment for the people driven into exile in Babylon, that they had to eat food which, by their standards, was polluted. And while such food was undoubtedly grown in dunged soil, it was not soiled by direct contact with it.

Part Three

Where there's muck there's brass

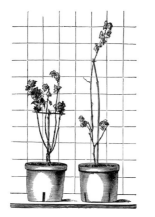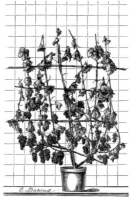

Vines grown in pots have different requirements from those in the ground or vineries. *Thompson's Gardener's Assistant*, 1900, demonstrates conclusively that pots without manure provided 'only a few shrivelled grapes'.

INTRODUCTION

Who was that, you rogues, that dung'd his own cap at stocks-market, and carried home the old gold to enrich his radish-bed?

John Norden, The Surveyor's Dialogue *(1607)*

The old adage 'where there's muck there's brass' dates from the seventeenth century. Interestingly some sources say that the origins of the word ordure are linked to *or* – the tincture gold or yellow in armorial bearings; others believe it is derived from *ord*, meaning filthy, foul. Manchester is noted for its soft water and the abundant rainfall on which its manufacturing fortune was founded. The French political writer Charles Alexis Clérel de Tocqueville visited Manchester on his travels through England and Ireland, after which he published *Voyage en Angleterre et en Irlande de 1835*. In the book Manchester attracts the following philosophical entry:

It is from the midst of this putrid sewer that the greatest river of human industry springs up and carries fertility to the whole world. From this foul drain pure gold flows forth. Here it is that humanity achieves for itself both perfection and brutalisation, that civilisation produces its wonders, and that civilised man becomes again almost a savage.

This is sewer as metaphor, but there was money to be made from dung if you knew where to invest it.

Whose dung is it anyway? In 1685 the managers of the Grosvenor Estate in London were asked to settle the vexed question as to whether a tenant or his landlord owned the dung. Their judgment? That 'the Cucumber Hole may bee lawfully taken away by him that layd itt there, But as for the dung in ye Ridges itt ought to goe with ye land'. A century later they allowed a gardener to remove all his dung as long as he levelled any disturbed or pitted areas. In 1798 John Middleton included lists of expenditure and costs in the Neat House gardens, part of the Grosvenor Estate, in his detailed survey of agriculture in Middlesex. Rents were £6 to £7 plus the costs of intensive labour added a further £35 per acre, on which they put an estimated sixty cartloads at 5s per load, which added a further £7 10s per acre. One gardener with 9 acres ordered six hundred loads of dung every year which was 'brought from the stables, and shot immediately from the carts in which it is brought, into an oblong heap. To this is daily added, what is brought home in the carts on their return from Town.' Middleton was impressed:

> This land has been long, or perhaps longer, in the occupation of kitchen-gardeners, than any other land in Britain, and for a great length of time has been supplied with dung, as much in quantity, and as often repeated, as, in the opinion of the occupiers, could be applied with advantage to the crops . . . one thing they unanimously agree in, namely, that to dung plentifully, and with discretion to dig the soil well, and to sow good seed; is the only practice on which a reasonable expectation of good and plentiful crops can be founded.

In 1825, when Thomas Cubitt (later builder of Osborne House and the Crystal Palace) acquired the Neat House gardens for building, he had to pay a premium £12 5s an acre as against an average price of £10 13s 4d on the nearby Wise Estate. Middleton concluded his geographical survey with the notion:

> That gardening is not altogether an unprofitable concern (as Dr Adam Smith has represented it to be), we may have ample proof, both in Middlesex and Surrey. There are generally some gardeners in the commission of the peace. It has produced several sheriffs of counties; and more who have realised from 20 to upwards of 50,000l [pounds sterling] in addition to their patrimony.

In 1807 Viscount Palmerston wrote about having to sack his gardener Knight who 'had behaved excessively ill. . . . He had not only neglected the kitchen garden and pleasure grounds at Broadlands but had plundered them of many valuable trees and shrubs, [and] carried away flagstones, dung, etc. for himself and his friends.'

Countryside Books have produced an excellent series of books on regional privies, including *East Anglian Privies – A Nostalgic Trip down the Garden Path* (1995). Home for the author Jean Turner included an outside privy until 1966, when at the age of 24 she left home to find flushing facilities. Turner compiled various local stories, one of which echoes the Grosvenor House case. Mr Neave of Attleborough wrote: 'For years, my father emptied our skip [a large, galvanised, wide bucket] on a midden across the road where he had a horse and carriage hire business. It is interesting to relate that when he sold the business, the transfer of the deeds had a clause enabling father to use the midden for as long as he required it.'

There was certainly money to be made from market gardening, reaping the rewards of hot beds and farming practices such as folding, penning and spreading for bumper harvests and prize-winning pedigrees. Purveyors of dung were rarely rich and never millionaires until the value of nitrate-rich guano was discovered and became a world player in politics, intrigue and diplomacy. Just as the sugar and slave trades brought huge wealth to many an eighteenth-century magnate, so the importation of guano and the virtual slavery of its Chinese miners created fabulous riches for the Gibbs family. The old saying could perhaps now be updated to read 'where there's muck there's more than recycling'.

Today's reading is from the *Book of Corporate Life*: Chapter 1, verses 1–15:

1. In the beginning there was the Plan.
2. And then came the Assumptions.
3. And the Assumptions were without form.
4. And the Plan was without Substance.

5.   And darkness was upon the face of the Workers.

6.   And the Workers spoke among themselves saying, 'It is a crock of shit and it stinks.'

7.   And the Workers went unto their Supervisors and said, 'It is a crock of dung and we cannot live with the smell.'

8.   And the Supervisors went unto their Managers saying, 'It is a container of organic waste, and it is very strong, such that none may abide by it.'

9.   And the Managers went unto their Directors, saying, 'It is a vessel of fertiliser, and none may abide its strength.'

10.   And the Directors spoke among themselves, saying to one another, 'It contains that which aids plant growth, and it is very strong.'

11.   And the Directors went to the Vice-Presidents, saying unto them, 'It promotes growth, and it is very powerful.'

12.   And the Vice-Presidents went to the President, saying unto him, 'It has very powerful effects.'

13.   And the President looked upon the Plan and saw that it was good.

14.   And the Plan became Policy.

15.   And that is how shit happens.

9

HOT BEDS OF CONTENT

Hot-beds may be made an amusement, and are even things of real utility.

William Cobbett, The English Gardener *(1833)*

Force Fed

The Romans used a thick layer of dung under the soil to create artificial heat to protect plants against frost damage in their northerly territories and enable them to enjoy out-of-season fruit and vegetables. They applied fermenting dung for additional heat and then used *speculare* (an early form of glass) for forcing. Tiberius Caesar especially craved early cucumbers. Another method was to fill baskets with dung-enriched soil and plant them up; these baskets were then placed in the sun covered with *speculare* to retain the heat and taken under cover at night to prevent chilling. Wheeled trays are mentioned by Gervase Markham in 1613, which were put out in the sun during the day and pushed to a shelter at night.

According to *Le Jardiniere Solitaire,* or 'The Perfect Gardener' (1706) by François le Gentil:

> The Manner of Making Hot Beds . . . Grapes. The best dung to be us'd for this purpose in an earth naturally Hot, is that of Cows; but if it cannot be got, make use of Horse-Dung, but thorough-rotten, that the Heat of it may be extinguish'd. In wet and cold Earth use Horse-Dung half-rotten, and never that of Cows, because 'tis cold and consequently bad for those sorts of Earths.

Meanwhile Philip Miller, in *The Gardener's Dictionary* (volume 2, 1748), recommended:

HORSE-DUNG is of great Use to make Hot-beds for the raising of all Sorts of early Garden-crops, as Cucumbers, Melons, Asparagus, Sallading, Etc. for which Purpose no other Sort of Dung will do so well, this fermenting the strongest, and, if mixed with long Litter and Seacoal Ashes in a due Proportion, will continue its Heat much longer than any other Sort of Dung whatsoever; and afterwards, when rotted, becomes an excellent Manure for most Sorts of Land, more especially for such as are of a cold Nature; and for stiff clayey Lands, when mixed with Sea-coal Ashes, and the Cleansings of London Streets, it will cause the Parts to separate much sooner than any other Compost will do; so that where it can be obtained in Plenty, I would always recommend the Use of it for such Lands.

The first extract given above was written by a Carthusian monk advising a French gentleman on gardening, while a decade earlier

Mrs Loudon, in *The Ladies' Companion to the Flower Garden*, did not shrink from the efficacy of 'thoroughly decomposed stable-dung' in floriculture, even using it to help half-hardy annuals overwinter.

in England the melon hot beds at Hampton Court Palace had doubled up as heated nursery beds for the exotic plants collected by William and Mary. The second extract is from 'Philip Miller FRS. Gardener to the Worshipful Company of Apothecaries at the Botanic Garden, in Chelsea'. Miller's *Dictionary* was read by many influential people, including the Revd Gilbert White of The Wakes, Selborne, a passionate grower of melons who also kept a *Garden Kalendar* from 1751 to 1768. Miller had supplied White with melon seed which he disappointedly noted 'produced abominable fruit'. Miller devotes nine and a half pages to 'Melo' and one of my favourite extracts concerns seed preparation:

> But if you cannot obtain Seeds of that Age, and are obliged to sow new ones, then you should either carry it in your Breeches Pocket, where it may be kept warm, . . . two Months before it be sown; by which means the watery Parts will be carried off, and the Seed prove equally as good as if it had been kept two or three Years. . . .

White experimented for five years before writing to ask for advice. Miller then sent him what he considered the best, 'cantaleupe' seeds from Armenia, with the advice that dung rather than tanner's bark should be used in the hot bed. The written word failed again so, on 23 June 1750, White journeyed to Chelsea to take first-hand notes of the correct procedure. Later that year White's *Kalendar* joyfully records that his hot bed too had produced 'fine, large beautiful fruit, just like Miller's'.

Hot beds started in trenches until observant gardeners noted that the shallower the trench and the higher the pile, the greater the heat. This is because dung tends to compact in trenches, whereas piling it up encourages a better flow of oxygen and greater fermentation resulting in increased heat. In 1660 John Evelyn illustrated his unpublished 'Elysium Britannicum' with hand-lights (cloches), cold-frames that look like a bottomless box made out of iron frame windows, and a four-poster bed reinvented as a curtained seedbed. These 'lights' were placed on the hot beds to enclose the heat, although horticultural glass was still in its

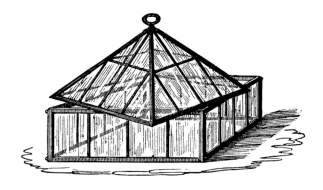

infancy a hundred years later. The life of a hot bed was about two months but Miller described an easy way to keep up the heat: 'When it begins to cool, cut away the Sides of it slope-ways, and laying fresh Dung to them, it recovers its Lost Heat, which is call'd Backing or Lining of a Bed; and this Work skilful Gardeners will repeat some-times five or six times in a Season, as they see occasion, rather than make a fresh bed.'

Neat Dung

Half a mile away in Pimlico the Neat House gardeners whose livelihoods depended on market gardening could not pay their rents in 1745 because 'it is a dismal Year among them, not having saved any Cucumbers or Melons'. However, with judicious use of dung and hot beds they could command premium prices for their early and out-of-season crops. Back in the 1670s Leonard Meager in *English Gardener* commented on the exceptional skills of London gardeners and their 'great Garden-grounds in or near London, where their grounds are in a manner made new and fresh once in two or three years, by dung and soil, and good trenching; so that their ground is as it were new and fresh for one and the same kind of Crops every year'. Writing anonymously in 1684 the 'Compleat Tradesman' thundered: 'And verily the vanity of some deserves our wonder, who are of that Heliogabalian

Stomach, to which nothing doth relish which is not dear . . . onely loving Pease, when they are scarce to be had.' Forty years later Miller commented on how they raise precocious peas on hot beds to have them early in the spring: 'they make an Hot-bed (in proportion to the Quantity of Peas intended), which must be well worked in laying the Dung, that the Heat may not be too great: the Dung should be laid about two Feet thick, or somewhat more, according as the Beds are made earlier or later in the Season; when the Dung is equally levelled, then the Earth . . . must be laid on about six Inches thick . . .'.

Their efforts were worth it, as can be seen by Richard Bradley's reports in *A General Treatise*: 'May 1723 . . . Forward Pease were sold this Month for Half a Guinea per Pottle-basket . . . Colly-flowers of the right sort 5*s* . . . June 1723 About the Middle of the Month, most of the Crops of Pease and Beans about London were ripe, and came daily in such Quantities to the Markets, that their Price was reduced to about one shilling per Bushel.'

The taste of peas freshly harvested from your own garden is delicious but we have lost the real excitement of seasonal fare now that frozen peas and petit pois are always available.

Manured Sperage

Asparagus remains a status vegetable and one that is almost seasonal. John Gerard, barber-surgeon and probable friend of Shakespeare, had over a thousand varieties of plant in his Holborn gardens, and he also gardened for William Cecil in London and at Theobalds. Describing asparagus in his *Generall Herball or Historie of Plants*, he calls it the 'manured or garden Sperage'. Around London many acres in Battersea and Deptford were dedicated to asparagus, but the premium prices were not gained for the main crop. John Worlidge, writing in 1675, offered a new technique: 'If you take up the old Roots of Asparagus about the beginning of January, and plant them on a Hot Bed, and well defend them from Frosts, you may have Asparagus at Candlemas [2 February], which is yearly experimented by some.' By the 1680s asparagus was four times as valuable as spinach or onions to the London market gardener. However, back to Deptford and Sayes Court, where one of London's most famous residents, John Evelyn, lived, gardened and wrote *Acetaria* in 1699. In his preamble he wrote: 'Sallets in general consist of certain Esculent Plants and Herbs, improved by culture, industry and art of the gardener.' Asparagus is described as 'Cordial, Diuretic, easie of Digestion, and to Flesh, nothing more nourishing. I do not esteem the Dutch great and larger sort (especially rais'd by the rankness of the Beds) so sweet and agreeable, as those of a moderate size.'

In 1767 John Abercrombie published the first edition of *Every Man his own Gardener*, being a 'New, and much more Complete Gardener's Kalendar Than any One hitherto published'. Abercrombie had grown up in East Lothian working in his father's market garden, but when they fell out he moved south to seek work. He wrote: 'Many of the kitchen-gardeners about London begin to make asparagus hot-beds about the middle or latter end of September, or early October, in order to have asparagus fit to gather by Lord Mayor's Day, which mostly happens the second week in November.' Incidentally the 'floats' used today for processions and pageants have their origin in the decorated barges that progressed down the Thames for the early Lord Mayor's Shows.

Shirley Hibberd, who lived in Lordship Terrace, Stoke Newington, with his wife and parrots, has already been mentioned. Apart from editing the *Gardeners Magazine* and publishing *Rustic Adornments for Homes of Taste* for aspiring Victorian urban gardeners, he also published *Profitable Gardening*, which was redolent with manurial advice for those seeking financial reward. In its illustrations it maintained the spirit of backyard enterprise, with one example depicting cats breaking the greenhouse glass and tumbling on to hothouse plants. Asparagus cultivation received seven pages, including a section on forcing by cunning means. The advice on pits had barely changed from that of the previous century, but for added measure the diligent gardener is advised that 'as soon as the shoots appear . . . give regular waterings of tepid liquid manure'.

Shirley Hibberd's magnificent 'summer cucumber house', the narrow span-roofed 'Paxtonian', as illustrated in *The Amateur's Greenhouse and Conservatory*.

The English have a preference for green, slender spears, but freshly gathered the fat, meaty white stems provide a veritable feast. Should any English readers wish to unshackle their prejudices and roll up their sleeves, they could try Hibberd's recipe for the 'German Mode' of growing asparagus:

In Germany this vegetable is grown with great care in order to produce it both white and eatable almost the entire length. It is always grown in deep, light, sandy soils; strong loams and clays are considered quite unfit to produce it. The ground is well drained, and dug to a depth of three feet, and a thick layer of horse-dung is put at the bottom of the trench, and mixed with the soil. Strong three-year-old plants are planted in furrows two feet apart, the plants being also two feet apart in the furrows. The planting is done in March, and the

167

plants grow without covering till November, when the soil taken out of the furrows is thrown over them, and the bed levelled. In February the ground is covered with a thick coating of cow-dung, the shoots appear above ground as the season advances and are cut at sunrise or sunset in lengths of nine inches. Asparagus grown this way, without forcing, is much esteemed; and so much care is taken to prevent deterioration, that it is never kept more than a day before being cooked, and is never put in water to keep it fresh for cooking. In districts where manure is plentiful, summer crops are grown between the rows of asparagus.

Discontent

The resolution of a bizarre legal case in 1685 concerning the ownership of stored dung is quoted on pages 157–8. It defined the finer points of a cucumber hole as opposed to a cucumber hot bed. A cucumber hole was exactly what the name suggests. About a bushel of soil was excavated and replaced with 'warm stable-dung' into which three cucumber plants with their own 'mould' were planted. However, in 1623 a spotted fever outbreak in London was blamed on 'the extraordinary quantity of cucumbers this year, which the gardeners, to hasten and bring forward, used to water out of the next ditches, which this dry time growing low, noisome and stinking, poisoned the fruit'.

Philip Miller was an early exponent of using tanner's bark in hot beds 'especially for all tender Exotic Plants or Fruits, which require an even Degree of Warmth to be continued for several Months, which is what cannot be effected by Horsedung'. However, he regarded the traditional horse-dung hot bed as essential for his readers 'to enjoy so many of the Products of warmer Climates'. Heat from these designer dung heaps was also ideal for raising seeds and gourmet crops such as kidney beans, which in March 1723 sold at 2s 6d per dozen but were available by the hundred in June for a mere 3s or 4s. John Middleton described in 1798 how 'by an union of natural fertility with heat (raised by dung), and a degree of moisture [he was] enabled to raise the greatest crops in the least possible time'. William Cobbett wrote in *The English Gardener* (1833) that dung was only fit for hot beds, and soil should be fed with prepared manure (or what we would call compost).

Hot beds are no longer a thing of the past. In the wake of the kitchen garden restoration movement visitors can see traditional hot beds in action at various places, including the pineapple pit at the Lord Leycester Hospital in Warwick. Meanwhile, a revival in the growing of specialist vegetables, combined with an interest in recycling and harnessing natural power, has spawned detailed instructions for making and using hot beds in various gardening books, magazines and papers.

Bed and Board

The wealthy and aristocratic in northern climes on both sides of the Atlantic prided themselves on enjoying out-of-season fruit from their gardens, particularly having strawberries for Christmas. Walled gardens were built with integral chimneys and great attention to aspect, and a team of expert gardeners managed the numerous glass structures within. Philip Miller devoted fifteen pages to 'Walls', opening with: 'In the building of Walls to accelerate the Ripening of Fruits, there have been many Contrivances for obtaining the greatest Warmth from the Sun'. Perhaps referring to his circle of fellow Scots, his final note on the subject read:

'There are some Persons near London, who make it their Business to produce early Fruit to supply the Markets with; which they perform by the Heat of Dung only, having no Fire-walls in their Gardens. The Method which these People follow, is to have a good Quantity of new Dung laid in an Heap to warm . . . they lay it close on the Back-side of their Fruit-wall, about four Feet thick at the Bottom, and sloping to about ten Inches or a Foot thick at the Top. This Dung should be gently beat down with a Fork, to prevent the Heat from going off too soon; but it should not be trodden down too hard, lest that should prevent its

Heating. The Outside of the Dung should be laid as smooth as possible, that the Wet may run off more easily; and if there is a Covering of Thatch, as is sometimes practised, it preserves the Dung from rotting too soon: by which means the Heat is continued the longer. The Time . . . End of January. This first Parcel of Dung will continue warm about a Month or five Weeks, when there should be a fresh Supply of new

carpenter or joiner. A portable greenhouse has lately been constructed in France of metal or earthenware, which consists of a stand or frame in which a lamp is placed, over which is a small cistern for hot water; and over this is a circular basin filled with sand, in which the pots are placed. The whole is covered with a hand-glass, and can be carried about from place to place: the only expense is the oil for the lamp.

The simplest kind of greenhouse is one only heated by manure, which, with the shelter afforded by the glass, is sufficient to grow grapes, and to force flowers, so as to have roses and lilacs, &c., at Christmas. The outer appearance of this house is very plain (see *fig.* 31); and it may be constructed

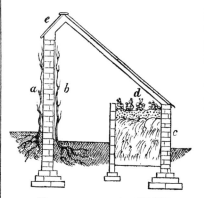

FIG. 32.—GREENHOUSE AND VINERY INSIDE.

stituted for them. A common greenhouse, heated by hot water, is shown in *fig.* 33, which contains a propa-

FIG. 31.—GREENHOUSE AND VINERY OUTSIDE.

at very little expense. There is a wall in front (shown at *c* in *fig.* 32) within which a dung bed is formed,

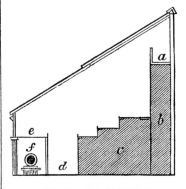

FIG. 33.—A SMALL GREENHOUSE.

The repeal of the Glass Tax in 1845 and a ready supply of dung revolutionised domestic exotic gardening.

Dung prepared, and the old taken quite away, or mixed up with this new Dung, to renew the Heat; which, if it works kindly, will be sufficient to last the Season. These Walls are covered with Glasses or Canvass, in the same manner as the Fire-walls. . . . Care must be taken to open the Glasses against these Walls, whenever the Weather will permit; otherwise the Steam of the Dung will occasion a great Dampness through the Wall; which, if pent in about the Trees, will be very pernicious to them, especially at the time they are in Flower.

He continued with words of warning over the difficulty of obtaining enough new dung, and suggested the cheaper option of wooden fences rather than walls.

Vineries evolved from the late eighteenth century, ranging from magnificent glass structures to the compact 'Curate's Vinery', but large or small the pattern of the glazed sloping roof along which the vine branches were trained was the same. The front of the brick base was arched to allow the vine roots to be trained away from the glass, exposing them to frost and liberal dressings of dung. This rich ground was also ideal for early salad crops, a system revived and perfected in the organic walled garden at Audley End in Essex.

On a domestic scale piling up dung around a rhubarb forcer (or a disused china lavatory pan) protects and feeds the rhubarb, encouraging the palest pink tender shoots. I tried the same trick with small pots over French bean seeds – but it just attracted every dormant insect on my patch.

10

REAPING THE REWARDS

Be avaricious for manure, and always keep your mind in firm conviction that your ground is in an impoverished state.

Shirley Hibberd, Profitable Gardening *(1855)*

Wise Investment

Pliny described a vineyard owner made wealthy eight years after thoroughly dunging his vines and having 'huge and mighty heaps of grapes' to the envy of his neighbours. The reward for Romans who had served twenty-five years in the army was to retire to their *villa rustica* and farm. This agrarian lifestyle was eulogised in *The Georgics*, a poem of 2,188 lines written by Virgil covering everything from the cultivation of crops to vines and trees, including the olive; farm animals; and bee keeping. A more practical approach to farming and gardening advice was also adopted by Roman writers: Cato (234–149 BC) produced *De Agricultura* and Columella *De re rustica* in about AD 60, while in 36 BC M. Terentius Varro wrote for his prospective widow *Rerum rusticarum*, a manual on agriculture that he hoped would help her in the running of his properties, which included an ancestral demesne at Reate (Rieti), a luxurious farm at Casinium (Cassino) and villas at Tusculum and Cumae. Palladius's later (fourth-century) writings on husbandry were largely based on Columella. All these works were in turn translated and adapted by eighteenth-century estate owners.

A rich seam of humour. *(The Museum of Garden History)*

Physical labour, often in the form of growing and harvesting crops, was part of many monastic lives, but the abbots and bishops of the medieval church eagerly sought the more gentle sensual pleasures of the garden. About a mile from Westminster Abbey the church owned a moated house with five gardens, in the sub-manor of Neat, which was frequented by abbots and kings. The property's deed of surrender in 1536 describes 'All that site, soil, circuit, and precinct of the Manor of Nete within the compass of the moat, with all the houses, buildings, yards, gardens, orchards, fishings, and other commodities in and about the same site'. In his fascinating book *The Neat House Gardens* Malcolm Thick traces the evolution of the property from an ecclesiastical rural retreat to the richly fertile market gardens that have already been described above. The earliest gardens straddled the banks of the Thames, enabling the easy importation of dung from London's privies and streets and the exportation of fruit and vegetables. As the number of market gardeners grew, they developed their own network of lanes and paths to the river. Many of the leases that survive include details of 'lay-stalls' where dung was stored, the value of which was such that the gardener would remove it when his lease ran out.

Eighteenth-century writers increasingly encouraged farmers to read gardening manuals as the gardening approach could be adapted for farms to increase yields. In 1720 John Styrpe published *A Survey of the Cities of London and Westminster*, which included a description of the Neat House gardeners 'keeping the ground so rich by dunging it [to] make their crops very forward to their great profit'.

Philip Miller of the Chelsea Physic Garden enjoyed international correspondence and plant exchanges, most notably with Carl Linnaeus in Sweden and John Bartram in Pennsylvania. Although a dung enthusiast (he recommended its use for heating up and feeding the soil), he also wrote about 'manures', or what today we would call home composting. Having extolled the virtues of bark, leaves, ditch weeds and shells, he concluded with the following observation on dung:

In dunging of Land, I have frequently observed in several Parts of England, but especially in Cambridgeshire, a very wrong Practice; for the Dung is laid on the Land before Midsummer, and spread abroad perhaps a Month or six Weeks before the Ground is ploughed; in which time the Sun exhales all the Goodness of the Dung, so that what remains is of little Service to the Land. Therefore when Dung, or another soft Manure, is used, it should not be laid on the Ground until the last time of ploughing, when it should be buried as soon as possible, to prevent the Evaporation of the Salts.

Farmers today have to 'inject' sewage into the soil so that none comes to the surface, mostly to prevent the anti-social stercoral stench.

Noblesse Oblige

The 'house of cards' hunting lodge at Versailles is embraced by magnificent gardens that mirror the power of the Sun King, Louis XIV. Its stellar creation was masterminded by a third-generation gardener, Andre le Nôtre and an army of gardeners. Still unsatisfied, Louis, king by divine right, also demanded an Edenic potager du roi within easy walking distance. For this he called on Jean Baptiste de la Quintinye, who in 1670 had been appointed 'Directeur des jardins fruitiers et potagers des maisons royales'. De la Quintinye had originally trained as a lawyer, but during a tour of Italy his eye for detail and delight in unusual tastes were captivated by gardening; as he later wrote, 'a good gardener must have a passion for novelty'.

Some 25 *arpents* (nearly 9 hectares) were enclosed. Le Grand Carré (Great Square), with a circular pool and fountain at its centre, was subdivided into sixteen geometric vegetable plots edged with clipped box. As the gardens were within easy walking distance of the château of Versailles, a raised terrace was created for the king and his visitors to view the living theatre of fruits, vegetables and, of course, the gardeners. This grand performance can still be seen today, with products to touch and taste. Le Grand Carré was surrounded by high walls, within which twenty-nine enclosed gardens created ideal microclimates for espaliered, cordon and free-standing fruit trees, soft fruit bushes and vegetables. Between 1678 and 1683 over 1,000,000 livres was lavished on the gardens, not least on Louis's favourite fruit, the fig. There were 700 different trees, some fruiting from mid-June onwards. Hot or long dung was readily available from the nearby stables, and this was supplemented with dung from beef cattle and dairy herds, used sparingly 'like monetary investment which replenishes the earth's treasure chest'. The use of dung, handglasses and the correct orientation ensured the production of fruit that ripened five to six weeks early, giving, for example, strawberries in March. De la Quintinye's *Instructions pour les jardins fruitiers et potagers* was published posthumously in 1690, and translated into English as *The Compleat Gard'ner* by John Evelyn. In Chapters XXII and XXIII – 'Of Amendments, or Improvements and Dungs' – he advised the use of all sorts of dung according to the temper and employment of the earth. He recommended large quantities for the production of pot-herbs (better known today as vegetables), but little or none for trees. Close scrutiny of the soil will reveal its defects, such as too much moisture or too little, coldness, heaviness or lightness. Ox and cow's dung he described as fat and cooling, that of sheep, horses and pigeons hot and light.

Regular Reaping

Thomas Coke of Norfolk created a 6-acre kitchen garden set within 14ft-high walls nearly a mile from his home at Holkham Hall. It was an ambitious precursor to the agricultural improvements he was to introduce across his Norfolk estate. Manure from his herds and horses, grazed, penned or stabled, was gathered and distributed across the estate and in his new walled garden. 'Long' and 'short' dung helped the gardeners to produce forty-five different vegetables and thirty-five different fruits for the kitchens. After Coke's death in 1842 a 120ft-high monument, surmounted by an enormous wheatsheaf, was erected to his memory, at a cost to his tenants of £5,409 19s 3d. The engraved stone tableaux around the base of the monument depict various rustic scenes: the Holkham sheep shearing, forerunner to our agricultural shows, with Coke himself and Earl Spenser inspecting the sheep; the irrigation scheme at nearby West Lexham; and Coke granting a lease to John Hudson of Castle Acre in Norfolk. The cornerstones depict the story of his progressive agricultural legacy: 'Breeding in all its Branches'

The wheatsheaf atop the monument to Coke of Norfolk, at Holkham Hall, who revolutionised farming practices, not least by popularising four-crop rotation.

The base of Coke's monument at Holkham Hall.

shows a Devon ox; 'Small in size but Great in value' shows a Southdown sheep; and 'Live and let live' and 'Improvement of Agriculture' show the latest plough and drill. All these improvements were assisted by his adoption of four-crop rotation.

John Norden surveyed the village of Barley in Hertfordshire between 1593 and 1603, noting that the village disliked the visits of their new king, James I, as he commandeered all their farm horses for his own use. Using Norden's own maps a further study was undertaken in the 1860s, by which time the four-crop rotation was well under way and the first bagged guano had been applied to the land. In 1864 in nearby Royston a company was formed to manufacture phosphates from coprolite diggings in Cambridgeshire. John Burgess personified the successful Barley farmer with some 339 acres, of which 239 acres were arable. He had 70 acres of wheat, 74 of barley, 64 of roots (including the brand-new mangel wurzel) and 66 for leguminous crops. By diligent husbandry and enthusiastic dunging he finally achieved a five-crop rotation: wheat was sown in the autumn, followed by barley in the spring and roots for sheep in the summer, and the corn was threshed in quiet moments always selling the first cut! The ewes were folded on to the roots during the winter, on to trefoil in the spring and on to the hayfields later in the summer, after the second cut of clover or sainfoin, but always keeping some for hay to feed his sheep or bullocks. The Royston Fair was held on the first Wednesday after 11 October, at which up to 400 bullocks would be shown and sold. Burgess was a regular customer, walking his animals back to Barley and overwintering them on straw, into which they obligingly trod their dung for spring distribution. Burgess, his contemporaries and their successors continued this model method until the First World War.

Paper Riches

Eating a fibrous diet is certainly good for the bowels but there's more to it than that. Its great potential for papermaking became apparent when Sheila Cooper and her family were examining a rhino midden in KZN game reserve in South Africa. 'Dung-blonde' is how Mark and John Cooper describe their mother, and her life has been ornamental and fertile. An artist in her own right, her work has encompassed recording Bushman rock engraving, teaching and papermaking. Based at Sedgefield in South Africa, Sheila, Mark and John established Scarab Paper, which is manufactured by recycling paper into which the sanitised fibre of elephant, rhino and other wild herbivore dung has been added for textural and visual effect – how appropriate that their trading name recognises the artistic skill of the dung beetle. A team of skilled local South African women handmake the paper in a series of at least twelve processes, and Sheila's art-work is printed and embossed on to the final product. Scarab Paper remains the only business that prints multi-lith, full colour artwork on to handmade paper. The process is very specialised and difficult because of the different thickness and texture of each sheet of paper. Sheila's latest project involves moulding and deeply embossing the paper, on to which she either paints or adds decorative artefacts to create a new and original expression of her passion for Africa.

Bayete Impressions is a special partnership with the World Wildlife Fund – South Africa, raising funds and promoting the conservation and protection of South Africa's biodiversity. The project is selling a limited edition of 'The Universal Elephant Footprint' embossed into elephant dung paper. Harry, an elephant from the Knysna Elephant Park, had the sole of his foot painted so that a monoprint could be taken. It is evocatively described: 'In spite of the untold billions of elephant tracks that have trod our earth over past eons, this is a contemporary image with an abstract quality.' The texture looks good enough to eat, while the greetings card called the 'Little Five' plays on the names of Buffalo Weaver, Leopard Tortoise, Elephant Shrew, Rhino Beetle and Ant Lion: 'The varied environments and diets of these animals make each sheet of paper unique.' Their envelopes bear the age-old insignia of the scarab.

The Not so Little Book of Dung

First find your elephant dung – and then process it into paper. *(© Bayete Impressions)*

Next decorate it with the cast of a wild track print from a waterhole in the Caprivi Strip in South Africa, and add further textural effects from films and photographs. *(© Bayete Impressions)*

Harry the elephant had his sole painted for a monoprint. *(© Bayete Impressions)*

Envelopes made from elephant dung posted the sixth-form students at Writhlington School into the finals of the 2005 Young Enterprise competition held at the University of Bath. Trading as Los Amigos del Bosque, they won the Fiscal Properties Shield for Best Product, the Systemagic Trophy for Best Use of IT, the Connexions West of England Shield for Best Stand, the Lloyds TSB Shield for Best Report and the HSBC Cup for Best Overall Result. The money raised is being used to support a school in Costa Rica that a group of the students had visited on a science expedition.

Under the compelling headline 'Roo poo hits the shelves, no messing' in February 2005 Charles Starmer-Smith reported that writing paper was being made from kangaroo manure in Tasmania. It is the brainchild of Creative Paper Tasmania, which is trying to create eco-friendly paper products containing no woodpulp. After the first batch of pulp-free paper was dispatched, they confessed that gathering an adequate supply of kangaroo and wallaby dung was going to be a problem. Joanne Gair told the *Advocate* newspaper in Tasmania: 'At the moment we are finding it very difficult to get the quantity of poo we need. We are hoping the community will help by collecting it for us and dropping it off in plastic bags. New or old, we'll take it all.' It would seem they need to recruit urban and suburban dogwalkers. Creative Paper Tasmania estimated that about 55lb of kangaroo manure can produce 400 A4 sheets of paper, and the plan is to produce post-cards in the future. Each of the sand-coloured sheets will be embossed with the words 'Genuine Kangaroo Poo', to prevent any fakes flooding the market. Maybe they should jump at the opportunity to ask Los Amigos to pack their trunks for a joint venture.

Another Great Aussie Salute

The happy union of Cootaburra and the African dung beetle was introduced in Chapter 4. The town's website now records that 'dung beetles are widely hailed as saviours by people, now able safely to open their mouths during summer for the first time in their lives'. In a bid to encourage visitors to the town, Cootaburra has launched a massive advertising campaign and also constructed a monumental dung beetle out of ferro-cement and fibreglass. Should you still choose to drive by, this giant beetle is visible from the highway as it stands almost six storeys high on a low hill and at night it is floodlit. There is even a hatch in the continually rolling dung ball so that you can climb into the hollow centre for a true coprophilic experience.

Inspired by this, the town of Yandackworroby developed a smaller model of the beetle, where the dung ball is the barrel of a stone rumbler, in which stones are rolled with abrasive powder until they are polished smooth as glass. Cootaburra now also has three of these rumblers polishing gravel from the Corella river into souvenirs, alongside dungball ear-rings, key rings, teaspoons and dung beetles in snowstorm domes.

Within minutes of an African elephant defecating, dung beetles fly in to roll away the mess and put it to good use. The efficiency led to their introduction into Australia in 1967.

11

MINING THE MUCK

Master Gibbs made his dibbs, Selling the turds of foreign birds

Rich Pickings

For three hundred years Spain and Portugal dominated the politics and mercantile trade with South America. In 1790, just two years before the Columbian triennial, Antony and Dorothea Gibbs celebrated the birth of their second son William in Cadiz. Antony had grown up in Exeter where he had been apprenticed to a merchant who specialised in exporting local woollen cloth to the Spanish mainland, the ships returning laden with produce from both the Iberian peninsula and the Spanish colonies. Sadly, he was somewhat overambitious, and his mercantile ventures led him (and his family) to bankruptcy. But with his expertise and knowledge of the lucrative South American trade, Antony decided to move his family from Devon to Spain. Despite the after-effects of the French Revolution, poor harvests and outbreaks of plague, followed by the struggle between the armies of Napoleon and Wellington, trade was brisk through Malaga and Cadiz (which was protected by the British Fleet). Although he was educated back in England, young William grew up to be bilingual in both language and business practice.

In 1808 Antony finally returned to London and established a new trading company, Antony Gibbs & Sons, at 13 Sherborne Lane off Lombard Street. After 1813 William returned to Cadiz to take advantage of the golden trading opportunities between Spain and her South American colonies. William set up two trading houses,

Antony Gibbs & Sons & Branscombe, and later, in 1818, Gibbs, Casson & Co. in Gibraltar. Both companies worked with Antony Gibbs & Sons and used his cousins' vessels out of Liverpool and Bristol. William then returned to London and during the 1820s, working with his brother Henry, established trading posts in Lima, Santiago and Valparaíso, taking advantage of the break-up of the Spanish colonial empire.

Rich in nitrates, guano had long been used by the Peruvian peoples, and now their new government gave itself a monopoly in both its excavation and its trade. Always seeking new trading potential, the Gibbs shipped a small quantity into London. Unfortunately it proved unmarketable, and they finally threw it into the Thames. Having had their fingers burned, they returned to less innovative but more profitable cargoes. By 1832 Antony Gibbs & Sons was the principal London trading house on the Pacific coast.

Concurrently with Antony Gibbs's business ventures, farming practices after the 'Agrarian Revolution' had been transformed by a Norfolk landowner, Thomas William Coke, better known as Coke of Norfolk. Coke had inherited the Holkham Estate in 1776, and he and his neighbour 'Turnip' Townsend introduced the new four-crop rotation of wheat, grass, barley and turnips. This brought to an end the need to slaughter herds at the outset of winter. Now they could be fed through the winter months with turnips until grazing was available again. But not even Coke's pioneering, enterprising work could halt the 1839 trade depression, nor prevent the poor harvests in the early 1840s. These, combined with the Irish Potato Famine and the threat of the repeal of the Corn Laws, brought about an agricultural depression. Four-crop rotation plus further improved fertility were urgently required on both sides of the Atlantic.

The newly founded Peruvian government negotiated for financial stability by means of long agreements, and Gibbs had to commit the company to a five-year contract to buy guano. In the year of Coke's death (1842) the first shipments of guano totalling 129,900 tons were shipped from Lima to the London docks. George Gibbs, a cousin near Bristol, agreed to show solidarity by testing guano on his land at Wraxall – and was rewarded with a marked increase in his wheat yields. British farmers began clamouring for guano, which was more productive than other natural fertilisers, and cheaper. Sadly Henry Gibbs died the same year, and never saw the enterprise take off. The following year William Gibbs published *Guano: Its Analysis and Effects Illustrated by the Latest Experiments* on behalf of the company. It began:

> Sir. Being largely engaged, as Agents to the Peruvian and Bolivian Governments, in the recent introduction into Europe, from the west coast of South America, of the manure GUANO, we beg leave to lay before you the following particulars and experiments, which we trust will prove interesting and useful to you. Of the genuine articles, imported by ourselves, we have deposits on sale both here and in the hands of our friends Messrs. GIBBS, BRIGHT AND CO., of Liverpool and Bristol, deliverable from the Import Warehouses.

It was all coming together. The transport system across pastoral Britain had also been undergoing major transformations, initially

Selected constituents in one ton of poultry dung, in one ton of farmyard manure, and in one ton of guano.				
Excrement of—	Nitrogen.	Potash.	Lime.	Phosphoric Acid.
	lbs.	lbs.	lbs.	lbs.
Hens, ...	43	19	58	39
Pigeons, ...	47	25	44	41
Ducks, ...	27	13	23	31
Geese, ...	15	21	13	12
Farmyard Manure,	10	12	39	6
Peruvian Guano,	156	67	269	314

The dung of fowls is a manure somewhat analogous to guano, although the food of hens, pigeons, ducks and geese is of vegetable rather than animal origin, while the seabirds that produced the guano lived on fish, and voided a more highly nitrogenised excrement. The guano became highly concentrated by the peculiar processes of slow decay to which it had long been subjected. (Table: *Thompson's Gardener's Assistant,* 1900)

with the construction of the canal network and later with the introduction of the railways. The early profits from their South American
ventures had allowed Antony Gibbs & Sons in London and Gibbs,
Bright & Co. of Bristol to raise the finance for Brunel's Great Western
Railway. By 1842 London had ceased to be a two-day journey from
Bristol, and ports could dispatch goods rapidly to inland warehouses.
William Gibbs's income soared, and between 1842 and 1875 the
annual partner's profits were as high as £100,000. Further
contracts were signed with the governments of Peru, Bolivia and
Chile during the 1840s and 1850s. By 1851 the Bolivian deposits at
Angamos were exhausted, but in 1852 Gibbs & Sons were able to
advertise themselves as 'THE ONLY IMPORTERS OF PERUVIAN GUANO'.

A Pattern of Islands

American historians charting the history of guano exploration and
exploitation define it as an analysis of nineteenth-century law,
sociology, geography, philosophy, biology and agriculture. American
farmers working along the eastern seaboard discovered that
scattered dried bird droppings dramatically increased crop production, thus creating a demand for guano all along the Atlantic coast.
Early guano was mined domestically from reserves in North
Carolina and other southern states. As the use of guano grew,
agronomists sought to discover why it worked, and scientists
showed that the value of guano depended on its potency. Different
varieties of guano were deemed better than others, based on the
amount of nitrates retained in the product. It was soon observed
that guano mined from exceptionally dry climates, where rainwater
had not flushed out the nitrates, was a far more potent fertiliser
than other more diluted phosphates. American farmers realised
they needed to locate and import rich guano from an alternative
source, and a series of investigative missions were instigated.
Peruvian guano was undoubtedly the best but the British had got
there first, and, having negotiated an effective monopoly, they were
in a position to charge accordingly.

Determined to get a foot in the door, the American Congress initially tried diplomatic measures, followed by a series of tariffs and incentives that proved ineffective with either the British or the Peruvians. In 1856 Congress passed the Guano Islands Act, signed by President Buchanan. It read:

> Whenever any citizen of the United States discovers a deposit of guano on any island, rock, or key, not within the lawful jurisdiction of any other Government, and not occupied by the citizens of any other Government, and takes peaceable possession thereof, and occupies the same, such island, rock, or key may, at the discretion of the President, be considered as appertaining to the United States.

America's finest cartographers and naturalists were hired by maritime speculators in the bid to claim uncharted fertile islands. Based on their researches, backers in Baltimore and other cities funded sophisticated and dangerous expeditions, mostly in the Pacific but a few in the Caribbean, the island of Navassa being the best known. Once 'discovered', these potentially rich islands challenged Congress, academics and the courts to protect them as new US possessions, along with the people who worked them. But it was a short-lived phenomenon. Before the close of the nineteenth century, synthesised fertilisers (especially nitrates) had become widely available and the importance of guano had passed.

The story of the guano gold-rush may have come to an end, but the aftermath has raised a few interesting footnotes. For example, during the Second World War some of the islands acquired under the Guano Act became tactically important during the struggle against the Japanese. It has also been alleged that these former guano islands were used during the Cold War to set up listening posts around Cuba and Nicaragua.

Inferno

The three stages of the guano trade, mining, shipping and marketing, provided nineteenth-century earthly illustrations for the fourteenth-century journey through the three realms of the afterlife, Hell, Purgatory and Paradise, so vividly portrayed in Dante's *Divine Comedy*. This narration and guided tour of the world beyond as a metaphor of humanity's ignorance and entanglement in the vices of the world was enacted by the people living in South America.

Dante's eighth circle of Hell was named 'Malbolge', or 'evil pockets', and consisted of ten circular tiered ditches separated by stone banks but linked by a succession of arched natural bridges. The canto opens with Dante's description of a grey stony place between a rock face above and a deep well below. In the first ditch horned devils whip former pimps in one direction while seducers and cheats are whipped in the opposite direction. The second ditch is filled with flatterers wallowing in pools of excrement, groaning, snorting and desperately trying to clean themselves.

The nineteenth-century grainy engravings of the guano mines match Dante's general topographical description, as do the harsh, brutal conditions of the miners, not sinners but slaves in the hands of latter-day horned devils. These conditions were unsparingly chronicled in Andrew Smyth's *Caesar's Passage*, set around 1864; the hero Milo Beran is a ship's boy from Sipan, Croatia:

'It doesn't get much worse than this,' said the lad, and they looked around gloomily. Beyond the shingle beach were row upon row of dilapidated houses. Crumbling masonry lay in piles, shaken off by previous earthquakes. The unpaved roads leading away from the docks teemed with people of all races, languages and colours, jostling and pushing, shouting, laughing and crying. Smoke from open fires swathed the sea front with pungent, acrid fumes [while] a damp mist cast a grey pall over the port and the hills of Lima, a few miles beyond.

'So this is what hell looks like,' said Arnie.

'How can they live with this disgusting smell?' asked Milo.

The lad laughed. 'You get used to it when you've been here long enough.' He paused. 'I suppose [you're going to the Chinchas?].'

'That's what the second mate told us,' said Arnie. 'What cargo can you get from an island?'

'Guano,' said the lad. 'You see the clouds of birds wheeling and diving before you even see the islands. There's so many fish in the sea the birds can eat all they want – and more. Doesn't matter how many birds there are, there's always enough fish for 'em. An' they leave their droppings all over. There's guano all along the coast south of here, but out in the Chinchas it's ninety feet deep in places. Just building up over hundreds of years with nothing to stop it. Fifteen years ago they took some to Europe and tried it out as a fertiliser, and it's been bedlam here ever since. They can't get enough of it.'

They relapsed into silence as they looked around the bay. Finally Milo asked, 'What d'you think our Old Man's doing ashore? Why don't we go straight to the islands and load up?'

'Gone to find some native Cholos to trim the guano in the holds, I expect,' answered the lad. 'Most sailors can't take the ammonia fumes – they make your eyeballs bleed unless you're used to it.'

The lad looked across towards [a] small ship, low in the water, weighed down by what seemed like a solid block of men. 'Chinese coolies,' he said. 'Brought across to work the guano deposits. They're on contract, but when they're on board they're locked up below decks for the three-month passage, just like cattle. Dozens of 'em never make it across alive.' He shrugged. 'Those are the lucky ones. You should see it out there – I don't think any of 'em lives long enough to finish the contract. Poor bastards. No one sees it as slavery, but it's difficult to tell the difference. They might be Chinamen, but they're still human beings. You'd never guess that the owners and Captains are all God-fearing men, taking money for cargoes like that.'

As the lighter approached, the overpowering smell of the dirty, emaciated bodies hit them, and they watched the sullen and silent workers pass by. The pale figures, covered in grime and filth, were still, staring vacantly ahead without emotion and without hope.

'What a place,' said Milo finally.

They were loading at the Chinchas for nearly three months. Milo watched moodily as crews from other ships organised boat races and fishing expeditions. He had never imagined there could be so many fish. They were packed so tightly that simply pulling a line through the shoal was enough to spear a mackerel on the hook. At night, the

American ships were lit up with coloured lanterns and the Captains' wives kept up incessant socialising and even dancing. Such was the huge demand for guano that there were close on three hundred ships at anchor around the three islands, either waiting their turn to be loaded from the main big ship chute, or ferrying the sacks and loading from hired lighters. On shore, Milo had watched the Chinese labourers work on the sheer cliff faces of white guano, digging and bagging amid the dust and overpowering smell of the deposits. Each gang was worked by an overseer with a twenty-foot whip which was used skilfully and instinctively, without thought or mercy. Many of the coolies threw themselves into the sea rather than continue with the hopeless misery of their situation, preferring to take an early release from the slow and wretched death from which there was no other escape. Milo couldn't understand how such conditions could be tolerated so unquestioningly, when slavery in America was being fought at such cost. He was sickened by the pretensions of the Captains' wives, whose attempts to maintain their own elegant society afloat was sustained only by the inhuman conditions ashore.

Paradiso

Gibbs's Spanish birth and upbringing endowed him with religious tolerance and a love for ceremonial expressed, for example, in his espousal of the High Gothic Style. His vast wealth enabled him to build Tyntesfield, described as a Christian house serving a Christian household inspired by the 'beauty of holiness'. How much did he know of the enslavement and diabolical treatment that laid the foundations of his God-fearing establishment? Much of Dante's *Divine Comedy* highlights the vices of the then universal Catholic Church; Gibbs and his wife Blanche became ardent supporters of the Tractarian or Oxford Movement, which claimed to encompass true Catholic worship without the corruption of either the Church of Rome or the Church of England. Intellectually and spiritually converted, the Gibbs used their fortune in many philanthropic ways. In London they worshipped with

Above the main entrance at Tyntesfield the devout Gibbs placed his motto, which translates as 'I place my trust in God'.

wealthy neighbours at St John the Evangelist's Church in Hyde Park Crescent; they became increasingly aware of the deprivations of their poorer neighbours to the north around Paddington, for whom they built a sister church, St Michael's, to minister to their needs – separate brethren? As well as rebuilding, restoring or supporting nineteen churches, Gibbs also helped the poor in his father's native Exeter, building the Exeter Free Cottages, four rows of almshouses in Tudor style. Gibbs's love of ceremonial was expressed not only through his religion and architecture, but also through the decor and books with which he surrounded himself. Throughout his life he worked with diligent industry and honesty. Gibbs, the great Anglican philanthropist, was known at work as 'The Prior', and his company's cable addresses were Genesis, Septuagint, Sadducees, Pharisees and Epiphany.

The magnificent estate at Tyntesfield was surrounded by ornamental gardens fed by guano money and possibly the product itself.

Fertile Follies

The guano industry has left three particular legacies around the world. The first is Clipperton Island, a barren, ring-shaped coral atoll no more than 75 miles across, located some 1,600 miles west of Nicaragua. The only atoll in the East Pacific, it serves as home for thousands of sea birds and millions of land crabs. Most of the island is no higher than 6ft, but Clipperton Rock, a volcanic rock formation, peaks at 69ft. The second legacy is Tyntesfield, that splendid Victorian High Gothic monument to fertile fortune, and the third is the SS *Great Britain*, the magnificent vessel that crossed the ocean between them.

Ferdinand Magellan discovered Clipperton Island in 1521, but it was later named after the English pirate John Clipperton, who led a mutiny against William Dampier in 1704 (and possibly buried his treasure on the island. If so, it has yet to be found!). In 1708 two French ships, *Princesse* and *Decouverte*, reached the island. Naming it 'Ile de la Possession', they annexed it for France. An American guano mining company then 'discovered' Clipperton and by a variety of legal and bullying tactics persuaded the French into agreeing to the United States having rights to guano mining there.

Neither the Americans nor the French established a permanent settlement on the island, so Mexico occupied the island in 1897 and established a military outpost there. In 1906 the British Pacific Island Company annexed the island and built a settlement in conjunction with the Mexican government in order to mine guano, and in the same year erected a lighthouse. By 1914 about a hundred men and women were living on the island, supplied with food every two months by a ship from Acapulco. This supply system broke down during the Mexican civil war and by 1917 the island's last three inhabitants decided to leave. In the late 1930s President Franklin D. Roosevelt considered making Clipperton Island an American possession with a view to using it as a trans-Pacific air base, and in 1944 he ordered the US Navy to secretly occupy the island. After the war it was abandoned, and it is now a French possession, visited occasionally by the French Navy and by the odd scientific or amateur radio expedition.

In 1850 Lawrence, Gibbs, Bright & Co. acquired Isambard Kingdom Brunel's mighty iron-clad ship, the SS *Great Britain*, a 3,500-ton vessel and the first five-screw steamship built for the Atlantic crossing. She had run ashore in Dundrum Bay near Belfast in 1846 so the new owners had to repair her. Initially she plied the Australia run, taking sixty-six days to reach Melbourne, but in 1876 she was switched to the new guano fields off Chile and the nitrate trade. After suffering damage off Cape Horn she was left in the Falkland Islands for many decades until she was repaired and returned to Bristol in 1970.

The mansion and estate of Tyntesfield has become a British treasure, saved for the nation as the embodiment of Victorian muck creating brass, translated into a bristling Gothic pile and its possessions. The majestic exterior of pinnacled towers, gables and

Our hero as modern art, toiling majestically up the slopes at Renishaw, Derbyshire, in 2005. (Artist: *Wendy Taylor*)

crenellations are matched by the splendid interior of vaulted ceilings, decorative carving, colourful tiles, water-closets and fabrics – the medieval court of the 1851 Great Exhibition and the power of the British Empire encapsulated into a single building. Outside, there were immaculate Italianate flower beds, landscaped trees and, just a short walk away, a walled garden containing an orangery and a vinery, along with the usual glass structures to re-create a fruitful Garden of Eden, fertilised probably with guano and certainly by the usual range of dung.

BIBLIOGRAPHY

Airs, M. *The Tudor and Jacobean Country House: A Building History* (Sutton, Stroud, 1995)

Amherst, A. *A History of Gardening in England* (London, Bernard Quaritch, 1895)

Anderson, A.W. *Plants of the Bible* (London, Crosby Lockwood, 1956)

Bacon, F. *Essays; or, Counsels Civil and Moral. The Colours of Good and Evil and Apophthegms,* 1625 (London, Seeley, Jackson & Halliday, 1872)

Beaver, P. *The Crystal Palace. A Portrait of Victorian Enterprise* (Chichester, Phillimore, 1986)

Bewick, T. *A General History of Quadrapeds,* 3rd edn (Newcastle upon Tyne, S. Hodgson, R. Beilby & T. Bewick, 1792)

Brawley Hill, M. *Furnishing the Old-Fashioned Garden. Three Centuries of American Summerhouses, Dovecotes, Pergolas, Privies, Fences & Birdhouses* (New York, Harry N. Abrams Inc. 1998)

Chaucer, G. *The Canterbury Tales,* ed. and tr. Neville Coghill (London, Allen Lane, 1978)

Cowper, W. *Poems of William Cowper of the Inner Temple, Esq.* (London, 1825)

Crocker, G. *The Gunpowder Industry* (Shire Album 160, 1986)

Darby, H.C. *The Medieval Fenland* (Newton Abbot, David & Charles, 1974)

Dawson, W.R. *A Leechbook or Collection of Medical Recipes of the Fifteenth Century* (London, Macmillan, 1936)

Díaz del Castillo, B. *The True History of the Conquest of New Spain,* 5 vols, tr. A.P. Maudsley (London, Hakluyt Society, 1908–16)

Elstobb, W. *An Historical Account of the Great Level of the Fens, called Bedford Level and other Fens, Marshes and Lowlands in this kingdom and other Places* (Cambridge, 1793)

Fabre, J.H. *The Life and Love of the Insect* (London, A. & C. Black, 1911)

Fiennes, C. *The Illustrated Journeys of Celia Fiennes 1685–c. 1712,* ed. Christopher Morris (London & Sydney, Macdonald & Co., 1982; Exeter, Webb & Bower, 1982)

Bibliography

Friend, Revd H. *Flowers and Flower Lore* (London, Swan Sonnenschien, LeBas & Lowrey, 1886)

Gottfried, R. *Epidemic Disease in Fifteenth-Century England* (Leicester, Leicester University Press, 1978)

Hall, A.D. *Fertilisers and Manures* (London, John Murray, 1909)

Halliday, S. *The Great Stink of London. Sir Joseph Bazalgette and the Cleansing of the Victorian Capital* (Stroud, Alan Sutton, 1979)

Hart-Davis, A. *Thunder, Flush and Thomas Crapper – An Encycloopedia* (London, Michael O'Mara Books, 1997)

Hibberd, S. *Profitable Gardening* (London, Collingridge, 1855)

—. *Rustic Adornments for Homes of Taste*, 1856, ed. John Sales (London, Melbourne, Auckland, Johannesburg, Century in association with the National Trust, 1987)

Higgins, R. *Greek and Roman Jewellery*, 2nd edn (London, Methuen, 1980)

Hogarth, W. *The Works of Hogarth* (London, J. Dicks, no date)

Jekyll, G. *Home and Garden* (London, Longmans & Co., 1900)

Johnson, G. *The Cottage Gardener*, 2nd edn (London, 1852)

Johnson, S. *A Dictionary of the English Language*, 2 vols, 6th edn (London, 1785)

Kevill-Davies, S. *Yesterday's Children. The Antiques and History of Childcare* (Woodbridge, Antique Collectors Club, 1991)

Kilroy, R. *The Compleat Loo. A Lavatorial Miscellany* (London, Greenwich Editions, 1996)

Kipling, R. *The Years Between* (London, Methuen, 1919)

Lambton, L. *Temples of Convenience* (London, Gordon Fraser, 1978)

Legman, G. (ed.) *The Limerick* (New York, Bell Publishing Co., 1964)

Lloyd, N. *A History of the English House* (London, Architectural Press, 1931)

Marshall, R. *In the Sewers of Lvov. The Last Sanctuary from the Holocaust* (London, Collins, 1990)

Miller, J. *Fertile Fortune. The Story of Tyntesfield* (London, National Trust, 2003)

Miller, P. *The Gardener's Dictionary In Three Volumes*, 3rd edn (London, John & James Rivington, 1746)

Milton, J. *The Poetical Works of John Milton* (London, 1811)

Norden, J. *John Norden's Survey of Barley, Hertfordshire 1593–1603*, ed. J.C. Wilkerson (Cambridge, Antiquarian Records Society, 1974)

Opie, Iona and Tatem, Moira (eds) *A Dictionary of Superstitions* (Oxford and New York, Oxford University Press, 1989)

Osborn, A. *Shrubs & Trees for the Garden* (London, Ward, Lock & Co., 1933)

Parker, R. *Town and Gown* (Cambridge, Patrick Stephens, 1983)

Powell, J. and Gribble, F. *The History of Ruhleben* (London, Collins, 1919)

Singer, A. *The Backyard Poultry Book* (Dorchester, Prism Press, 1976)

Smyth, A. *Caesar's Passage* (London, Calypso Press, 2002)

Strong, J. *The Exhaustive Concordance of The Bible* (Iowa Falls, Riverside Book and Bible House, 1980)

Switzer, S. *The Practical Kitchen Gardener* (London, 1727)

Thick, M. *The Neat House Gardens* (Totnes, Prospect Books, 1998)

Turner, J. *East Anglian Privies* (Newbury, Countryside Books, 1995)

Valliant, G.C. *Aztecs of Mexico*, rev. Suzannah B. Valliant (London, Book Club Associates, 1975)

Wotton, H. *The Elements of Architecture* (London, 1624)

Wright, L. *Clean and Decent* (London, Routledge & Kegan Paul, 1963)

INDEX

Index

Index